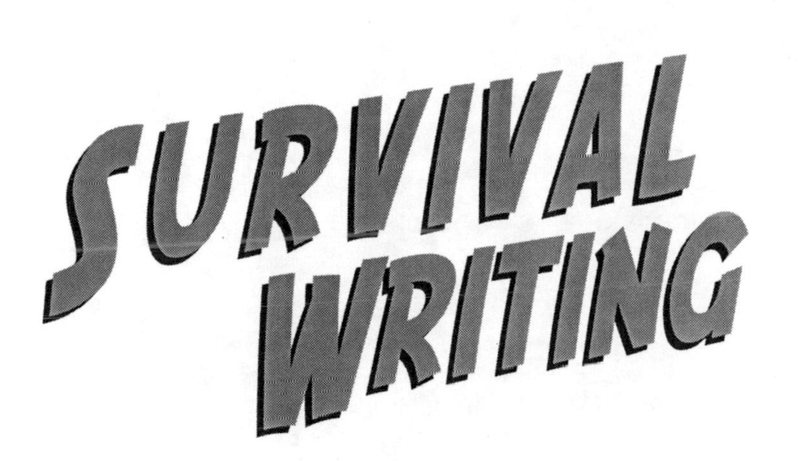

(HOW TO WRITE LETTERS, RESUMÉS, PITCHES, INVOICES, EMAILS, ARTICLES, REPORTS, AND EVERYTHING ELSE YOU NEED TO KNOW HOW TO WRITE.)

CLAIRE SCRIVENER

CHESHIRE HOUSE BOOKS
NEW YORK

CHESHIRE HOUSE BOOKS
P.O. Box 2484
New York, New York 10021

COVER ILLUSTRATION: Sam Ryskind

DESIGN & PRODUCTION: Bernard Chase

ISBN 9780967507323

LIBRARY OF CONGRESS CONTROL NUMBER
2009928706

FOREWORD

Like learning how to build a fire without a match, or find North without a compass, or why not to argue with a stranger who's called The Hulk, learning to write well can be a basic tool of survival. You need to— in fact you simply have to know how to write. And no, we're not talking about The Great American Novel. More likely we're talking about the Great American Email, or the Great American Resumé , or the Great American Term Paper, Letter or Report. Learning to write them well can be your passport out of the wilderness and into the stuff you want: the job, the opportunity, the customer, or the check.

This book, then, is meant to be a primer on writing well and a guide for applying it to necessary, practical, everyday uses.

It's based on a college course I'd given at The School of Visual Arts in Manhattan, and originally designed to help students on the verge of being deported into the world. These were students of all ages— from the 18-to-20's to the newly divorced 40's to the newly retired adventurers embarking on third careers. Then, too, it was crafted from the lessons I learned the hard way, not only as a writer (both staffer and freelance) but as a sometime entrepreneur— those painfully gathered lessons about the prose (and the cons) of contracts, the trouble with presentations, the armor against thievery, the secrets of getting paid.

May you master them all the easy way.

And so, let's begin....

CLAIRE SCRIVENER has written "something of everything"—19 published novels and novelizations, television dramas and documentaries, magazine journalism, newspaper book reviews, advertising copy (at 4A agencies and, later, freelance), and lyrics, sketches and special material for nightclubs and Off-Broadway. She has also taught writing and literature courses at The School of Visual Arts in New York City where she currently lives.

FOR MORE INFORMATION
ABOUT THIS BOOK
WWW.SURVIVAL-WRITING.COM

CONTENTS

PART I: WRITING

1

WRITING IS A PROCESS, NOT A LEAP OF FAITH

Aside from graffiti, almost everything you write— a paper for a class, a letter for a job, a pitch for a project, a proposal for a grant, or even the most ordinary email to a client— will always have one really dreadful thing in common: it will all require writing. Even worse, *good* writing.

Which means, among other things, logic, organization, clarity and brevity.

And since good business writing, like good classroom writing, begins with good writing, let's talk about writing and what makes it good and how to make it happen.

I know. This is hard. There are a lot of people for whom the mere sound of the word "writing" is like the sound of a dentist's drill. Say the word "writing" and their teeth begin to hurt. Imply the word in a sentence, like "Your paper is due tomorrow," and they're gripped with a sudden urge to...defrost the refrigerator...visit a sick aunt...even *go* to the dentist— anything to delay that impending moment of doom, that collision between the blank page and the blank mind.

If your teeth, even now, are beginning to feel funny, I'd like to suggest you change— not your feelings about writing— but your whole approach to the job. To begin with:

DON'T THINK OF WRITING AS WRITING.

I am not being precious. Nor am I instructing you in games to play with your head. I am not saying, "Don't think of broccoli as broccoli." Broccoli *is* broccoli, and there's nothing much you can do. But writing, as a pure matter of practice, isn't writing. And a lot of your vexing problems come from wrongly thinking it is. But when you actually get down to it—

WRITING IS THINKING, AND WRITING IS TALKING.

Writing as thinking takes a bit of elaboration, but writing as talking comes to one simple rule:

NEVER LET SOMETHING COME OUT OF YOUR PEN THAT WOULDN'T, EASILY, COME OUT OF YOUR MOUTH.

If you wouldn't *say* it that way, don't *write* it that way.

A lot of people get into trouble with writing because they wrongly believe that it's different from speaking. That what you're supposed to do is to translate your thoughts into some kind of foreign language called Writing.

Don't do it.

Writing is not a foreign language. It is not a Second Language. It is not a different language.

If you approach it as though it is, you are going to drown. You are going to choose words whose meaning you aren't sure of because they're words you never use. And, even worse than that, you'll get all tangled up— and obscure your meaning— in the desperate convolutions of a sentence structure that has never, in your life, passed between your lips. (And likely for good reason.)

Don't do it.

Test drive all of your written sentences. Say them aloud (read them to a tape recorder or a friend). If your friend says, "Huh? Whaddaya *mean* by that?" and you can explain it to him quickly and clearly with your mouth, listen to what your mouth said and write it like *that.*

The acid test for any sentence is this:

IF IT SOUNDS PECULIAR, IT *IS* PECULIAR. GET RID OF IT. THROW IT OUT.

Writing, at least on a fundamental level, is just talking with your pen. And looked at in that way, the only important difference between talking and writing is that once something's spoken, it can't be erased. All you can ever do is pile more words on top of it in an often desperate effort to clarify or explain it.

But once something's written—as long as it hasn't been handed in or mailed—you have a cool second chance. You can clarify it *before* you've officially said it. You can say what you *should* have said, or what you *wished* you'd said, or what the you in your movie-version self *would* have said. Beautifully, cleverly, and, best of all, briefly.

A question that can logically arise from that premise that writing is like talking, is "Yeah, okay. But suppose I don't talk well?" Okay. Suppose. The difference is that talking with your mouth is instantaenous and can happen faster than thought. Which can either leave you blathering and blurting idiotically or else leave you um-ing till the postman arrives from your head. But writing is thinking *first*, and if you think you've written it awkwardly the first time you wrote it, you've got a second, third, ninetieth...or as many times as you give yourself to try to say it better.

If by "not talking well" you mean your grammar becomes approximate, okay, you can fix it. And, for hard fact, you must.

If Writing Is Like Talking, Bad Grammar's Like Bad Breath.

And so is bad spelling. They're totally irrelevant to your talent as an artist or your worth as a human being, or the worth of your ideas, but you'll be judged by them anyway, and the world is too hard, fast, cold, and competitive to go around promiscuously creating a bad impression. Correct grammar requires study; correct spelling's an easy ace. If you can somehow never remember whether an "absence" makes the heart crave a second *s* or a *c*— at least remember you never remember and bite the bullet and look it up. How much trouble is hitting Spellcheck? Or (*here's* a thought) how about the Dictionary icon? Or (steady now) how about the actual paper book?

The best reason to use the book (whatever life form it may assume) is that, unlike the Spellcheck, it astounds you with proper meanings and with models for proper use.

Did you say "disinterested" when you meant "uninterested"? Did you perpetrate "evolvement" when you struggled for "evolution"? Did you simply make up a word? Clue: When you can't find a word in the dictionary, it's probably not a word.

Let's get back to the beginning.

Learning to write well, in itself, gets divided into two separate skills— Process and Technique.

If you hate (*hate*) to write, if the thought of having to put something down on a piece of paper puts your stomach into a knot, then it's probably because you haven't learned Process.

So let's talk about Process.

Beginning with the fact that:

WRITING IS A PROCESS.

It's not *one* step, it's several.

One of the things that likely kicks your stomach into your shoes is the fact that you *believe* that it's all one move. That you're standing on the edge of a skyscraper roof looking over at another roof 60 feet away and you think you have to get there in one hard terrifying leap across the void.

And the fact is, you don't. The fact is you get there by: going down in the elevator, walking 60 feet, and going up in the *other* elevator.

And once you know that, your stomach feels better. And not only that, but you know something else: That everybody else has to do the same thing.

There is no sane shortcut.

The fact that you have to parcel it into several separate steps instead of one inglorious leap is not because you're cursed to be exceptionally inept...but because *that's the only way the job is ever done.*

Now—when we talk about the Process of Writing, what we're really getting into is a Thinking Process.

WRITING CLEARLY IS THE END RESULT OF A LONG PROCESS OF THINKING CLEARLY.

And again, it's a "process." Nobody arrives at clear thought in an instant.

Edison did not just suddenly greet morning with a lightbulb in his head. And Michelangelo did not climb the scaffold to that ceiling and just start to ad lib.

Edison did hundreds of experiments first, and painters do dozens of preliminary sketches. And so do most writers.

The reason you do a preliminary sketch is to corner those elusive little glimmerings in your head and try to make them concrete, so you can actually, visually *see* what you were thinking. Once it's on paper, your *sub*jective thought becomes an *ob*jective thing and now (and only now) you can look at it objectively, *see* what's wrong with it, and start to make it right.

Doing something wrong, then, is not a waste of time; it's a necessary step on the way to get-it-right.

Or another way of saying that (at least very often) you can't do it right until you've done it wrong.

And to nail that down:

YOU CAN'T WRITE UNTIL YOU KNOW WHAT YOU WANT TO SAY, AND YOU CAN'T KNOW WHAT YOU WANT TO SAY UNTIL YOU'VE WRITTEN SOMETHING DOWN.

Writing, in itself (at least in its first stages) is nothing but a *part* of the process of thinking. Or to put that better:

WRITING DOWN YOUR THOUGHTS IS THE FIRST STEP IN THE PROCESS OF MAKING THEM CLEAR ENOUGH TO BE WORTH WRITING DOWN.

Therefore, consider:

The first things you write will be always and only your notes to yourself. A record—an objective record—of your thoughts. And your first thoughts, at that.

Only when you've got them in a form where you can see them can you start to refine them—or decide they're total drivel and think another thought.

One of the greatest errors that people make in writing is that after they've heroically written something down, they believe it's what they think, believe it's *all* they think, and further believe that while it isn't very good, it's the best they can do.

Wrong, wrong, and wrong.

So let's delve into Process as a way to make it right. And let's begin by applying it to:

LONG FORM WRITING:
ARTICLES, BUSINESS PRESENTATIONS AND REPORTS

Step One of the process is simply:

1. THINK (AND MAKE NOTES ABOUT YOUR THOUGHTS)

And to start with, relax. Just because you're holding a pen in your hand or your fingers over a keyboard, you are not in danger of Writing. You're thinking-and-making-notes.

Repeat after me: "I am not writing." Now try it a little louder: "I AM NOT WRITING!" There. Feel better? Because actually you're not. Step One isn't writing any more than making a shopping list before you head off to the supermarket is writing. And *because* you're not writing — *because* you don't have to worry about the words—you can concentrate on thinking.

Think about your subject. Think longer and harder than you usually think. Push yourself. Hard. Stick a flashlight into your ear and flash it into all the little potholes in your head. If you see an idea there, grab it by the neck. If it hollers, it's alive. Rassle it out of its hidey-hole and slap it onto the page.

And every time you're certain there's nothing else in there, make another trip. Ask yourself sternly and firmly, "What else?" In fact, *write* "WHAT ELSE?"—right there on your page and then force yourself to answer it. Stare at that question impolitely for 20 minutes before you allow yourself to write the word "Nothing."

My experience in teaching is that people invariably know more about a subject than they put into their papers. But your job in a paper is to put it all down. The assumption is: you *have* put it all down, so you're judged by what's there—and *only* what's there. So too, in real life. Your proposal for a project has to stand on its own as it travels to many desks, and goes to many meetings as your sole representative. *Get it all down.*

Step One, then, is crucial. You know *what* you're doing (you're jotting down your thoughts; you're collecting the raw material for your project; you're forming, at least vaguely, what you *think* you want to say) but how do you do this Step One doodling?

Any way you like. Any way that works.

Let's assume, for the sake of argument, that the job is complex. That it requires you to summarize or otherwise distill a whole gamut of information and form it into a thesis. The model for all this would be a term paper for college. Remember the way you dealt with all those term papers for college? Or let me put it this way: Remember the way you *should have* dealt with those papers? Very well then, let us review.

You can start with a simple **list**. List everything in your head: Facts, ideas, possible ideas to think about later. Opinions, generalizations, anything that moves.

You can do your list tersely. **Key words** can be enough. Like a shopping list: "Milk, soup, eggs" can be enough. *You* know what you mean so you can go back later and get more specific. (Gallon of organic 2% milk; Campbell's Tomato Soup...)

Or: ramble on. Follow a thought for as long as it itches. **Free associate**. Play. Start to write one thing and drop it for another if another comes to mind, no matter how tangential or unrelated. Just take it as it comes.

But the rule is to

**WRITE DOWN EVERYTHING YOU THINK
AND EXACTLY AS YOU THINK IT.**

Some of what you write in these first random notes could be beautiful, precise, exquisite sentences you'll wind up using in your final piece of work.

Some of what you write could be muddy, ungrammatical misspelled bilge.

Don't worry about it. Don't go back and correct it. Just keep making notes.

Some of what you write may strike even you as being dumb and irrelevant, but just keep writing. Pretend you're a stenographer with a very dumb boss.

Your only job is to take dictation.

If as soon as you write a thing you see that it's wrong or see an argument against it, don't cross it out, write *why* you think it's wrong. Because all of this is helping you to know what you think, or to *discover* what you think.

Let's say you're reviewing a movie. Your original assertion is "It wasn't convincing." Well, okay, but you can't hit-and-run. As your reader, I'll demand to know *why* it's unconvincing— or why *you* think it is. (I mean maybe you personally think it's unconvincing because, in it, a sailor sails around the world, and you believe the world's flat. So you have to say Why.)

In fact, I'd even suggest that while you're marshalling all your arguments, you also write down— on a separate piece of paper or the palm of your sweaty hand—

THE NEWS QUESTIONS:
WHO? WHAT? WHERE? WHEN? AND WHY?

And maybe, for good measure, add HOW? FOR EXAMPLE? and even our old nagging friend WHAT ELSE?

Why?, however, is the question to ask first. Pretend there's a prosecutor sitting on your desk who keeps hitting you with WHY?

You're reviewing this movie. The only thing you know when you first sit down to think is the raw gut assertion:

*"I really didn't like it." (**Why**?)*

*"It was dumb." (**Why**?)*

*"It didn't make sense." (Specifically **where** didn't it make sense?)*

*"In the graveyard scene."(**How** didn't it make sense?)*

*"It didn't make sense because the girl went to the graveyard alone at midnight when she knew the vampires and the werewolves were there, and she'd otherwise shown she was really pretty smart." (**When** had she shown that?)*

"When she found the sunken treasure."

The point is, you already knew those things, but you forced yourself to think them. And once you've thought one set of fully coherent thoughts, you've learned how to encourage yourself to think a few others.

But caution: Don't go to the opposite extreme and start over-explaining. If you say "the sun rose" this is not a time to ask yourself *why* the sun rose. So the rule of thumb is:

IF AN INTELLIGENT PERSON COULD REASONABLY AND SOBERLY ASK YOU SUCH A QUESTION, ASK IT YOURSELF. (IF ONLY AN IDIOT WOULD ASK IT, MOVE ON.)

Among the things I've written are television documentaries and magazine articles, both of which bear a rather frightening resemblance to term papers in college. And they follow the same rules. Part of my Step One entails going over my notes (going over them with a highlighter, or bolding important parts if my notes are on the computer) and then, after that, making notes on my notes— pulling out the stuff that seems interesting and important; making parallel notes on what I'm *thinking* about my notes. Like how the material possibly fits together; how it proves or disproves a case; how it jibes with the rest of the world; how it jibes with the rest of my head— what values or insights or opinions the stuff evokes.

But at this point in the process, it's still only notes. You're still not writing; you're just talking to yourself. So write to yourself the way you'd talk to yourself— in whatever kind of language you talk to yourself in.

I mean, if you're thinking "Oh [Bleep], that's wrong," write: "[Bleep], that's wrong."

I am not here suggesting that you actually hand your boss a lot of [expletive deleted] but I *am* suggesting that you

START TO SMASH THE WALLS BETWEEN THOUGHT, SPEECH AND WRITING.

Or to put that in reverse, that you

START TO FORM BONDS BETWEEN THOUGHT, SPEECH AND WRITING.

But at least for the moment you are not writing.

What you might want to do to remind yourself of that is to remove yourself—physically—as far as you can—from your usual scene-of-that-crime called Writing. So you might want to do this, not at your desk, but on your bed or your sofa with a notebook and a pen. Try it. See if it works.

And as long as I'm flacking for PaperMate and Bic, I'd like to extol the virtues of the spiral notebook. (Your pages stay in order, and none of them gets lost.)

The point is: relax. The freer your mind is— of pressures, discomforts, strains and distractions— the better it'll work.

And distractions include music and television sets. You know how a lot of really sub-moronic lyrics can sound almost witty when they're set to a good tune? So can moronic thoughts. You have to be able to listen to your thoughts against dead, blank silence.

Okay, let's talk about the goal of Step One. What you're doing here is literally

GATHERING YOUR THOUGHTS.

If instead of a piece of writing, somebody'd asked you to do a crayon drawing, Step One is the equivalent of gathering your crayons. Seeing—objectively—what you've got to work with. But don't look at them now. When your thoughts are all gathered, leave them alone to play. Wash your hair; wash the phone; take a break; you've earned it (and it's even part of the process). When you come back refreshed, you'll be ready for Step Two.

2. THINK (ORGANIZE, ANALYZE, DEVELOP WHAT YOU'VE GOT).

What you've got is a big messy jumble of crayons. If somebody'd asked you to do them a drawing, you wouldn't just hand them this dumb pile of crayons— because in that case you're asking *them* to do the drawing.

One of the biggest problems in most people's writing is that all it ever consists of is Step One Thinking— a random list of thoughts (a loose pile of crayons).

The point is, you want to *make* something of your thoughts, create something out of them. A point, a point of view, a theory, a pattern, an argument, a design. (These are your thoughts but *what do they add up to?* These are your crayons but what's The Big Picture?)

The first thing to do—especially if we're talking about a research paper—is to

ORGANIZE YOUR NOTES—
TO (OBJECTIVELY SPEAKING) ORGANIZE YOUR THOUGHTS.

And I'm talking right now about physical organization. You don't want your crayons in a big messy jumble so whenever you want blue you have to plow through the whole drawer. It's not only time-wasting, it's maddening.

So your first priority is to put together— in one place—all your notes about each of the different facets of your story.

Say I'm writing an article for *Food Fad Magazine* on "The Role of Fruit in Contemporary Life." I've done a lot of research. I've read a lot of books. I've interviewed a large, demographically-balanced group of contemporary fruit-eaters, and noted my own thoughts.

Now, reviewing the total mess, I find references to apples in interviews 1 and 8 and scattered among my book notes, so the first thing I want to do is to physically put them together. (And repeat the whole process with the mangoes and pears.) There are several ways to do it, and they're all a pain in the neck. If your notes are on the computer[1], you can open a new file, or simply copy (but don't move) all the apple-stuff in the lot. Just be sure that you add a note about whence (which interview or book) the stuff came. And always put quote marks around a lifted quote. If somebody else said it, the credit belongs to him. A lot of major writers who've been publicly nailed for plagiarism have used the "faulty note transcription" as their excuse. True, it can genuinely and innocently happen. But it's really *no* excuse. Any more than "I stole the car because I had to get to church." We'll talk about citations and their proper use later, but meanwhile: be scrupulously careful about your notes.

However I've done it, once I've got all of my apple notes together, I can see what they do— or don't— add up to. I can underline or bold the most promising passages. I can analyze what they mean. I can look for

---

1 No computer? Make a photocopy of your notes. Using the copy, and using a pair of scissors, cut out the stuff about each of your different subjects, doing them one at a time. Tape the cuts on a new page, each page with its own heading. (Oranges; Nectarines.) Or else: Just go over all your notes with a highlighter, using different color highlighters for each of the different subjects. Or else: just scribble the key words in the left margin; or resign yourself to your fate and retype it on a computer; and then take it from there.

the Golden Apple. Or the *seed* of a Golden Apple that I might want to develop. I can also look for the worms. Are apples, in fact, an interesting subject or are apples a dull thud?

But maybe when I look at my blueberry notes (now collected in one place) something hits me like a bolt:

I've interviewed seventeen people about fruit and nine of them repeatedly yakked about blueberries, and seven of those nine were a hundred years old and they all ate blueberries seven times a day.

So— ta-da! Maybe *that's* my story: "Blueberries, Key to Eternal Life!"

I'm making two points here:

The first is that simply by organizing, and then analyzing, my notes, I've created something out of them. From mere random thoughts— from lists of seemingly unconnected factoids—they've become an idea. And only now can I begin to *develop* my idea and to structure my article *around* my idea.

But the thing is, I couldn't even *get* the idea till I'd organized and, finally, analyzed my notes.

So the Process is a chain and everything you do becomes a necessary link.

The fact is we don't always know what we think— or even know what we know— we often have to discover it. As part of Step Two.

Shift gears for a moment.

Suppose what you're writing is an advocacy piece— arguing either for or against a proposition. Attempting to make a case. You've listed your arguments as part of Step One. Now it's time to develop them. To take all your talking points and deal with them one at a time. The order isn't important. (You won't *know* the order till you've finished with Step Two.) Pick a point, any point, and then follow it through to the end. Examine the reasons behind it. Explore its ramifications. Gather facts that will prove its premise. Find examples of how it works. Illustrate it. Analogize it. Assert convictions about it. Refine those convictions till they finally reach a point where they begin to sound convincing— or they utterly fall apart and you decide that they're not so convincing after all. Pretend you're the opposition. Can you knock the point down? And can you, as its advocate, defend it against attacks? If you can, then you might want to strike a preemptive blow and clobber the counter-arguments before they put on their gloves. Again, you're not writing, you're thinking and making notes. And beginning to get a clue about the strength and the ultimate position of each point within the framework of the whole.

And, not by the way, you'd follow the same process for a business presentation (an advocacy piece in which you're touting your own work).

I'd like to talk more about Step Two Thinking because it's really so crucial to everything you write. To *everything* you write— from a dashed-off memo to the slog of a long treatise.

What your readers are looking for— and looking for quickly— is the tag on The Bottom Line. They don't want to sit around and fiddle with all your factoids, they want you to add them up. And they want you blaze a clear, clean path to the final point.

In other words, they want you to ORGANIZE, THEORIZE, GENERALIZE, SUMMARIZE, ANALYZE, SYNTHESIZE and, ultimately, back your assertions with the facts.

Of the few mental talents you can teach yourself to acquire (by beating your head on a wall) one of the most useful is the power to

SUMMARIZE.

And we're talking summarization in its most refined sense: summarizing a summary. Boiling a thing down and extracting its very essence; doing a fast forward to the meat of the bottom line.

If the question is "What's the Constitution about?" the answer is *not* to copy down verbatim the first 8 articles and 26 amendments. It's not even to summarize, one by one, the first 8 articles and 26 amendments. It's to pull out the ultimate and absolute gist. Can you do it in a sound bite?

Yes, sure you can. In fact, you could manage it in twenty words flat (or in twenty flat words).

The Constitution is about: "establishing a governmental system of checks and balances which further balances the rights of the individual against the rights of the state."

That, or you could you could try it in forty very moving and memorable words:

The Constitution is about: "We, the people of the United States [attempting] to form a more perfect union, to establish justice, insure domestic tranquility, provide for the common defense, promote the general welfare and secure the blessings of liberty to ourselves and posterity."

Which is what the founding fathers said it was all about in their own Preamble to the Constitution.

Note: preamble. They prefaced the Constitution by telling you exactly what they were doing so you'd know what you were reading.

Learning to get quickly to the heart of a matter, to its overall point, is one of the most practical talents you can acquire. Because ultimately "What's the Constitution about" is exactly the same as a life-or-death pitch: What's your screenplay about? What's your resumé about? What's your project about, and why should we fund it, what's in it for us?

Another of the top ten tricks is to

GENERALIZE.

The dictionary tells us that generalizing is: *"To reduce to a general form; to infer an overall view; to draw a general conclusion from specifics."*

In exams I've concocted for literature classes I occasionally offer one of those "briefly discuss" questions, like: "Briefly discuss the overall image of women in the work of writer X."

And even though I give specific instructions ("*Don't* just give me the bios of the women, come up with a generalization") still, I get answers that, unhappily, go like this:

"The women X writes about are Ann, Joan and Sue. In the course of the novel, Ann kills Harry. Joan, a detective who knows what Ann did, confronts her, demanding $100 million as the price of shutting up. And after she gets it, Sue, her own sister, kills her for the money."

End of report.

What's wrong with that answer? It's Step One Thinking. It's a catalogue. A list.

Even if I didn't give specific instructions, the question implicitly begs you to generalize. To reach an encompassing overall conclusion; come up with a generalization.

So while you might want to deal with those gory specifics in your private Step One (as you'd write a list of numbers before you could add them up), now add them up! *Make* something of them. You've got a blackmailer and two killers. Add two killers and a blackmailer together and you get—

Three villains! Therefore:

"All of X's women are villains." Or "X doesn't seem to like ladies very much." And *now* you can back your assertion and move on.

And again, you've got a skill that's got practical applications. Drawing conclusions and stating them up front, making generalizations (as long as you back them up) is a great tool for selling.

Just for example:

"These 5 million photographs, taken in every country in the world, show women at work."

Publisher, gallery owner, has something to hang his hat on. He knows what you're selling him and further, has a handle on the way he himself can sell it to the public. Now. Right away. He doesn't have to puzzle over 5 million photographs and try to figure it out. And *you* won't run the risk that he'll *never* figure it out.

The alternative—in this case, the losing pitch— goes:

"Enclosed: 5 million photographs. 1) Navajo potters, 2) Vegas Strippers 3) Jamaican teachers. . ."

You can see where that's going and it's not going anywhere. It's Step One Thinking. Take it to Step Two.

And then you're ready for Step Three.

3. <u>Find A Structure. A Scaffold. A Logical Order For What You Want To Say.</u>

Before you can do that, you have to decide:

- What's the focus of what you're writing? (What's it about?)
- What's your overriding point?

• What facts—in diminishing order of importance—best help you to make it?

• What *other* points have you got? What best supports *them*? And how do those points contribute to your thesis?. . . and how do those points relate to one another?

Whatever you decide here, it isn't carved in stone but you have to decide something in order to start writing, and if only because:

YOU CAN'T REWRITE UNTIL YOU'VE WRITTEN.

(Whenever I've written something totally lousy, I console myself with that.)

In any case, keep in mind:

THE STRUCTURE IS ALWAYS A LOGICAL PROGRESSION.

In your Step Two thinking you've built a train of thought. But your train can't go anyplace until you've built a track.

Your structure is the track.

You know your destination and you have to build your track along a logical route that will get you where you're going. From point A to point Z.

You might plot your structure by doing a written outline. Or you might simply number your topics in Step Two in the order you *tentatively* think you'll introduce them— since you can, and you probably will, change your mind.

Something else to consider:

If your structure is a track, then you might want to build it on the geometric promise that the shortest distance (the most efficient route) between any two points is a rail-straight line.

But also consider this:

That Euclidean railroad isn't always necessarily the most scenic route —or the one that's the most fun. For your reader or even you.

So the point would be this: Your structure— your track— should be the rail-straight line. An arrow that moves cleanly from beginning to journey's end and is planted for all to see. And the train— your thesis— the burden of your thought—has to stay on the track or the results would be disaster. Derailment. Collapse.

But: If you want to, you can stop the train at a station— leave it on the track— get off, hitch a ride, and go merrily off on a tangent— as long as when you're finished, you get back on track.

The caution here would be: *Don't get sidetracked.* Don't wander so far from the station for so long that neither you nor your reader can easily get back or remember where you were going.

Another point about structure is the need for —

TRANSITIONS.

Think of transitions as the crossties on your track. They hold the track together and allow you to go smoothly from one section to another. (One thought to another.)

A transition can be as simple as "However," or "Then, too," at the start of a new paragraph. Or maybe it's just tacit— implicit in the logical juxtaposition of your thoughts. In the best of all writing, it *will* be implicit, so strive to make it so.

In any case, once you've got your tentative structure, you're ready for Step Four.

4. WRITE A DRAFT. (4A. REWRITE IT.)

I won't lie to you. You are now writing. But it's a totally different experience from what you've done before. Because you're not trying to write *and* think *and* organize *and* find a structure all at the same time. You've done all that.

When you've finished your first draft you won't (or you shouldn't) have a sense of completion. You're not home free, but you *are* out of the woods.

Now take a break. Have lunch, wash the dog. And then look at what you've written, *see* what's wrong with it (or what could be better), make notes on your critique, and then, when you're ready—the same day or the next—do your first rewrite. And note I said "first."

After that, take a break. This is urgently important. Run from your first rewrite as you'd run from a rabid cat. Don't touch it. Don't look at it. Stay away from it overnight so you'll protect yourself from the risk of falling fatally in love with it (since love, as you know, can be notoriously blind). Then look at it again in the chilly repentant light of The Morning After and—if you need to— do another rewrite.

But, please, I caution you:

Don't Overdo It.

Obsessively *re*-writing can become *un*-writing. And instead of making it better, you'll eventually make it worse.

Whenever you're relatively pleased with what you've done, leave it. Take a break. Overnight, if you can.

5. Polish (Edit)

Your goal is to clarify and simplify your prose.

There Are 4 Rules To Follow In Editing Your Prose:
Be Clear, Be Exact, Be Natural, Be Brief.

Your goal in writing is to put all your thoughts, quickly and clearly, into your reader's head. Both at the same time. Quick *and* clear.

Meaning: Take *out* extraneous words and lines; sharpen and clarify the necessary lines.

Refine your sentences. Chisel away the fat. If a word's just lying there—wasting your paper and wasting my time— then kill it without mercy. If you believe it's got a socially redeeming feature—that it illuminates, amuses, humanizes, possibly even kicks up the rhythm, then indeed, let it live.

Do any of your sentences feel like a life sentence? Do they ramble on and on? Do they wander over meadowland before they go out to sea? Does it occur to you somewhere in the middle of a sentence that you're suddenly embarking on a slick downhill road in a car without brakes and, even with catastrophe looming at the bottom, you don't know how to stop? Stop! Rethink it. After you've removed all the deadwood and the weeds and condensed all the blather, if you still can't control the thing, break it into two.

Your objective is always and foremost to be clear.

Clarity Is Your King.

Sacrifice any other pieces on your board to protect your king.

When you're editing you also want to shore up your structure. Ask yourself: Is it supporting your train of thought?

Your sentences and paragraphs now *are* your train. The paragraphs are cars and each of them is logically linked to the next one and the whole thing has got to be traveling somewhere.

Edit with a train master's sense of direction.

A good way to test the logic of your structure is to make what I call an **after-the-fact outline**. Go over what you've written, paragraph by paragraph, and list the points you've made in the order you've made them. Does the order have logic? (In your Beauty Tips article, did you tell me about unwanted hair on page 2 and then add another tweezing tip on page 17 in the middle of waxing wroth about toenail fungus?) If the order's without logic, change the order. Attempt to keep related information related, not whimsically scattered about. If you're making a point, make it— thoroughly and entirely— before you go wandering off.

Edit with your eye and then edit with your ear. Here's where you want to try speaking what you wrote. To yourself or, if you're seriously in doubt, to a friend. Is it totally, immediately clear to your friend? Ask your friend, earnestly, to tell you what you said. When you hear yourself say it, does it sound as though it actually came from a human being? From a human being you'd *like*? Have you said it on paper as you'd say it with your mouth? Forget what you've written now and *say* it with your mouth. If your mouth says it better, take dictation from your mouth.

Copy your final version. And again take a break. Overnight, if you can.

(I'm offering you an argument against crashing a deadline. Haste is your enemy. Time is your friend. The longer, and the further, you can get away from your work, the more objectively you can see it— till eventually you can see it with the reader's virginal eye.)

6. PROOFREAD.

Examine what you've written for technical errors: spelling, punctuation, grammar, typos and— crucially— missing words. Your mind tends to caret in the word that isn't there (most especially *and*'s and *the*'s). If the project's really important, get a friend to read it, too. Her mind is a blanker slate; her fresh eyes are a sharper tool.

7. Make It Readable.

First, neatness counts. For two reasons: It's harder and takes longer to read something messy than to read something neat. Make it hard for your reader and he may stop reading, or (at best) you'll tick him off. Which is not the kind of mood you want to put somebody in if you're writing to get a job. Or a check. Or an A. And second of all, the subtext of messy is messy. It says, "I'm careless and I couldn't care less," and your reader can assume that's the operative attitude in everything you do.

One way to make things easier to read is to simplify your layout. It should go without saying (though it rarely ever does) that you should double-space manuscripts and always leave a one-inch margin on all sides. (If your reader's making marginal notes, he needs a margin and, aside from that, the white space is comforting to the eye.)

Re-examine your long paragraphs— the ones that look to your reader like a school day without a recess. Break them up into smaller parts. This is not, however, a question of just hacking away at random. Be alert for the natural seams.

Be alert, in fact, for every chance to lighten your reader's load and to feed him with information. Small bites are digested best.

For example, consider

SUBHEADS.

What a break for the burdened eye! What a guide for the wandering mind!

—> Pointed bullets can be effective

—> Bolded phrases can have their place

Little boxes, in moderation, call attention to Something Big and cause your reader to pay attention.

Moderation, of course, is key. If you're cluttering up your pages with a series of noisy gimmicks, you'll have stepped on your own feet.

Okay; so that's it. You've completed the seven steps.

Asking how long it takes is like asking how long it takes to do a painting or find a mate. (Half an hour or half your life.)

RANDOM NOTES ABOUT RANDOM THINGS

There's a certain responsibility that attaches itself to writing. Most readers have inordinate faith in the written word. They'll believe, because *it's in writing*, that it somehow has to be true. That belief is supremely foolish but it seems to be wired in. So the thing of it is, unless you're really practicing to deceive, you owe a courtesy to your readers.

Facts Are Supposed To Be Facts.

When you aren't dealing with fiction, you're ostensibly dealing with facts, and you'd better make sure you are. Take nothing you say for granted. Always check to be sure it's true.

If You Don't Know A Fact—find It.

You can google at 3 AM; the public library's open at 9. But have you ever thought of the phonebook? It's an obvious fund of experts in whatever you need to know. Experts, as a genre, love to blabber their expertise and are flattered to have you ask them. You can find them at universities, or specialty publications, or cooperative corporations. Almost every organization has a public relations department, or a customer service office, or a bureau of press relations or a show-off with time to chat.

Interview. Ask. Stretch. Put some new information into your head so you can put some into your reader's.

Here's another random conceit:

WHATEVER IT IS YOU'RE WRITING, *YOU* ARE NOT THE SUBJECT; YOUR *SUBJECT* IS YOUR SUBJECT.

Even when you're asked to give a personal opinion, your opinion's not the subject. It's the camera, not the shot. The shot is what you're giving your opinion *about.*

For example: I've asked students to write critical reviews of the book they've just read. Below is the beginning of a paper I once got that was one page long and whose entire one page was no more or less informative than its two opening lines:

"The first two chapters were a little too slow and used words I didn't know. I didn't get interested till about chapter eight but then I really liked it."

All of which tells me nothing about the book but more than I want to know about the reader.

The subject of all her sentences is "I." The eye of the beholder is looking in a mirror at...the eye of the beholder and seeing nothing else. The student who wrote this wasn't reading the book, she was reading a thermometer stuck in her own mouth. Get *out* of your own attic. Get *out* of your own head. Get out beyond the foxhole of personal reaction.

Confer on your subject an objective reality, and then deal with *that.* (What's the book about? What's it *trying* to be about? What about its story line, characters, style. And then—in your opinion —did it fail or succeed. How? Why? When? Where?)

Similarly, when you're asked to critique a new accounting system for your office, or to offer your opinion on the value of someone's pitch or the kinks in the new insurance plan— remember: your subject is the system, the pitch, the plan.

IT'S A MATTER OF PERSPECTIVE

Let's say you're a camera and your subject is a cat. You can start with a tight close-shot—the cat filling the frame— and then gradually do a pullback.

Is the cat curled on a sofa? or on a box in a dark alley?

It's still the same cat but when it's suddenly put in context, it's a cat of a different color.

Pull back from it even further. Is the couch in a dark alley? (Did somebody get evicted, losing couch, cartons and cat?)

Again, it's the same cat. But the shots from the different angles lead to totally different statements about totally different things and their relation to one another.

Nothing is isolated, except, as we choose, arbitrarily, to crop it.

I'm not saying *don't* crop it.

Obviously, you have to. Otherwise every shot would be a shot of the whole universe, and every family saga would begin with Adam and Eve. I'm simply suggesting that you see where you are. That you think about context and grope for perspective. That you look for connections— within your subject, and between your subject and the doings of the world.

Broaden the general horizon of your thoughts.

What I'm not saying here is that you *must* find a bunch of connections or a theory or a Serious Social Statement.

If you don't find one, you don't find one. If the emperor looks naked, there's a hot chance he is. Nor am I provoking you to turn over your head to intellectual hallucinations. I'm inviting you to look. Look around. Speculate. That's a really neat word. It means "to think" and also "to gamble." I'm saying do both. I'm telling you to take a gamble on your thoughts. To take mental risks. Which will, after all, be the secret to your success: having your own perspective, having your own vision, and having enough faith to put it out to the world.

PROCESS

1. THINK (MAKE NOTES).

Free associate. List key words, ideas, points of view, quotations (with sources). In fact, write anything you find in your head. Then ask: WHAT ELSE? Don't criticize or edit. In a research paper, look over your written notes. Make notes on your notes and then proceed as above.

2. THINK (ORGANIZE, ANALYZE, DEVELOP WHAT YOU'VE GOT).

Organize your thoughts. Gather the evidence to back your assertions. Ask yourself the News Questions. Hunt for an angle. Generalize. Summarize. Theorize. Think. What's the Big Picture? What does your Step One stuff add up to? What single, overriding point do you want to make or point of view do you want to take? (Do you need to do any more research? Do it.)

3. THINK (DECIDE ON A TENTATIVE STRUCTURE).

Find a logical progression. Build your track. If you need to make a side trip, get off the train (go off on your tangent) but after you've finished, get back on the track. Don't get side-tracked. Check your transitions (the crossties on your track—the links between one subtopic and the next). Are they logical? Smooth?

4. WRITE A FIRST DRAFT (4A. REWRITE IT).

You're putting together, in a tentative structure, the sum of your first and your second thoughts. This is not cut in stone. It's possible you'll have to do 3 or 4 sketches before you get it right. If so, you may want to take some breaks in between. And try to take an overnight break when you're through.

5. EDIT.

Clarify and simplify what you've just written. Have you said *exactly* what you wanted to say? Have you said it as briefly as you possibly can? Remove the extraneous. Sharpen the necessary. Edit with your eye. Edit with your ear. Read it aloud to yourself or to a friend. Is it clear to your friend? Does your prose sound human? Does your structure have logic? Then, too, DO YOU LIKE IT? If you don't, try again.

6. PROOFREAD.

Check for grammatical errors; for spelling errors; for errant typos and words that aren't there. And remember: even Spellcheck won't help you out if you've used the wrong word or committed the kind of typo that itself is a word. Check your punctuation. Does it help your reader out or put hurdles into his path?

7. MAKE IT READABLE.

Is your type too dense? Could you break up your paragraphs without losing logic? Would subheads or bullets help make your points? Could you try a friendlier font? Careful, though. Don't get gimmicky with layout; gimmicks can distract.

GUIDELINES FOR STEP TWO

Consider these approaches to sophisticated thinking and focused organization

1. SUMMARIZE:

Condense. Extract the essence. Go for the hot heart of the matter. Beyond the details and the surface distractions: *What's This About?*

2. GENERALIZE:

Look for common denominators. Do isolated facts and specifics form a pattern? Look for the pattern.

3. ANALYZE:

Break things down to their elements. You've tasted the cake; can you tell what it's made of? You know the result; do you know how it evolved?

4. SYNTHESIZE:

Put the parts together in a new or original way. Tinker with the givens.

5. EVALUATE:

Make judgments; offer opinions. Find trends and relationships

6. THEORIZE:

Make suppositions. Consider: What if? Or: Where does this lead? Find an offbeat angle. Back it up with specifics to really slam it home.

7. THINK ABOUT CONTEXT (PAST OR PRESENT):

Look for connections—within your subject and between your subject and the doings of the world.

8. PLAY WITH PERSPECTIVE:

How would this look from a different point of view?

9. PIN YOURSELF DOWN:

Back your assertions. Test your assertions. Try to knock them down. If you can, reconsider them, or build a better case.

2
WORDS, WORDS, WORDS

In the beginning, there was the word.

God *said*, "Let there be light," and whammo! there *was*.

And whether or not you believe that literally, words are strong stuff. They create reality. We're not talking about God's words now, but your words... my words... their words.

By saying something *is*, you can make a thing *be*— or at least *seem* to be, whether or not it *is*. (Santa Claus; dragons; the emperor's new clothes.)

Further, my words— the words that I've just now splattered across the page or spoken into the air— now themselves exist. They're as real as a desk or a slam-dunk or a war. They're something that's *happened*.

You can quote them, if you want to, and report them in a newspaper, and whether or not I meant them, the fact is, I *said* them and the words in themselves have now become a fact— at least in the sense of "a thing that exists."

You can hold me to them legally. Called a verbal contract.

You can sue me over them. Called libel.

And I can sue *you* if I contend you misquoted me.

And if our case gets to trial, it'll be *your* word against *mine*.

Words are strong stuff. They can get you into (or out of) a mess.

If you say something cutting or hurtful to a person, your words can have the same reality as a blow. Or bring other people to blows. ("Those are fighting words, pal.")

Lies, come to think of it, are wholly composed of words, and every novel is just a lie—a clever protracted fiction built of black inanimate words. And yet the words can create worlds, alternative realities so real they can make you weep.

Propaganda is pulp fiction— a cheap, dirty trick of systematic falsification that's designed to arouse passion and create a political "truth" which itself, of course, is a lie.

But however you come to use them— for the pleasures of finding Oz or the nightmares of following Hitler— words, true or false, are the tools that define the world; and the stuff on the sticky labels that we use to define ourselves.

As perhaps they define the species. That all-important difference between us and the other apes.

There's the theory that postulates that language creates intellect, not the other way around. That you can't *have* intellect —the ability to think abstractly or profoundly—until you have language. So it isn't that man, of all animals, had intellect and therefore created language, but that man, of all animals, had language and that *language* created intellect.

And bringing that up from the caves to this minute, there's a psychological theory that if your language doesn't offer you the word for a concept, the concept doesn't exist. (If there isn't a word for it, you can't think it; can't think it, can't conceive it, so it doesn't— at least for you personally— exist.)

I'm not taking that to extremes. I'm not saying that if English didn't have a word for "mattress" that we'd never lie down. I'm referring to abstractions: the abstract conceptual complexities of life.

Just for example: There's an Amerindian language without a word for "time." And that particular tribe of Indians doesn't have the same sense of time as you and I. Their time-words are limited to "sunrise" and "moon," "snowfall" and "harvest." But they don't think of "time" as an independent concept: the stuff that goes on *between* the sunrise and the moon. And forget about "I'll meet you at 2 o'clock for lunch."

In Orwell's novel, *1984*, Orwell makes the argument that language itself is a political tool, and for just that reason.

His fictional government creates a new language, a language called Newspeak, which banishes words like Honor, Justice, Morality, Democracy, Religion and Science.

All of these are highly complicated words. Monumental abstractions. You can't point at Honor like you'd point at a chair. You can't either show or picture its existence, so Orwell was dealing with the same basic premise: that *if* these abstractions didn't have a word— couldn't be articulated even to yourself, let alone to your neighbors, they simply couldn't *be*.

Or to put that in absolutely practical terms:

If you can't *think* something, it follows that you can't either do it or be it or get it or have it. And the point is, you can't think it without the word.

The whole aim of Newspeak— of amputating the language— was to narrow the range of thought and the realm of possibility; to make political rebellion literally unthinkable and to cripple the human mind.

If You Stop To Think About It, Words Can, In Fact, Occur Without Thought, But Complicated Thought Can't Occur Without Words

There are two kinds of thinking that each of us can do:

Abstract and Concrete.

Or to put that another way: Word vs. Picture.

"Time" is abstract. It's a complicated concept that clusters around a word. A sidewalk's concrete. (You can picture a sidewalk; it's a simple concept that clusters around an image.)

Pictures are said to be worth a thousand words and very often they are— and just as frequently they're not.

Draw a picture of time. Not of clocks— of Time.

Draw a picture of justice—with no caption— and make me understand.

The word, in both cases, is worth a thousand pictures. Or infinite pictures.

If you want to know, approximately, the length of a thousand words, it's just about from here to the start of this chapter. And their purpose (at least their intended purpose) was to interest you in looking at words in a different way— to stop taking them for granted, to accord them great respect, to realize how urgently important they are— whether or not they *should* be.

In less philosophical and more practical terms, words are the basic tools of communication. And like any other tools, they have to be used properly.

Rule #1: You Can't Wing It With Words.

They are, or they're not. They're in the dictionary or they're not and if they're not, they're not words.

A dictionary is the most important book in any language. It's our book of common meanings; our book of common prayer. If somebody's written you a word you don't know— if they're in Maine with no phone, even if they're dead— you can still get their meaning if you cross to your bookshelf and look in that book. Universal decoder. Modern Rosetta Stone.

Technically, therefore, it's fair to use any word you find in the dictionary, and technically not fair to use a word that's not.

But the catch remains this:

You Have To Use The Word *As* The Dictionary Uses It. Exactly.

A student once wrote that "the hero was insensible." She meant "insensitive." "Insensible" means either A) unconscious, in the sense of passed out, or B) imperceptible— so insignificant that no one knows it's there.

You can't *do* that with words. They mean what they mean and only what they mean. Near-misses don't count. You can't be "a little right" like you can't be "a little dead."

If you're using a word you don't customarily use in the course of a conversation, check it out first.

Rule #2:
Just Because A Word *Is* In The Dictionary, Doesn't Mean It's Right Or Appropriate To Use.

Just because a pink tulle gown is in your closet, you don't necessarily want to wear it to the beach.

Don't get fancy.

Use Words To Communicate, Not To Show Off.

For one thing, the show-off approach can backfire. Instead of sounding more intelligent, as you'd hoped, you can wind up sounding idiotically pretentious. You can sound as though you're *trying* to sound elegant and tony. And that isn't what elegant and tony is about.

Elegance is simplicity.

Fancy is overdone.

Don't overdo it. Widen your vocabulary to make it more subtle, more supple, more exquisitely understandable, but not to make it fancy for the sake of being fancy.

RULE #3:
FIND THE EXACT WORD.

The reason there are 23 words in the language to describe a single action is that each of the 23 has a slightly different shading. Choose the right one and you can fine-tune your meaning or otherwise your tone.

The boy dropped the book out of the window.
The boy threw the book out of the window.
The boy tossed the book out of the window.
The boy hurled the book out of the window.

Each of those verbs has a slightly different nuance; each of them is useful in helping you to home in tightly on your image (and indeed, do it briefly).

The boy defenestrated the book—which means "threw it out the window" does absolutely nothing...except make me dislike you. Talk about tone. And while we're on the subject (of meriting animus)—

RULE #4:
AVOID JARGON.

A jargon, by the way, is a colorless smoky stone from which the verbal form of jargon apparently gets its name, or in any case ought to. Smoky and colorless about wraps it up. People who intend to be purposely obscure, to divorce their language from the realm of flesh and blood, to play inside baseball, or simply to elevate pretension to an art, are the world's most terrifying jargon abusers. Technobabble, cant, euphemism, nauseating waves of grandiosity are merely the outward symptoms; jargon is the disease.

People who write business letters and presentations seem to catch it like the mumps, their cheeks getting swollen from the mouthfuls of pure mush.

Somebody writes in a memo: *when you interface with clients...* and immediatly "interface" is everywhere you look. In your hair, in your craw and, even worse, in your mouth.

It's one form of jargon, and it's one of the very worst.

Parts of a machine can be said to interface (or fit back-to-back); you can interface (in other words, line) a skirt, and your computer can interface (connect) with your printer. Human beings, however, "get together and talk." More simply, they "meet." And even saying "meet face to face" is redundant.

Don't "implement" something; just plain "use" it.

Don't "maximize" something. "Make the most of it," maybe.

Don't "expedite" something; just "try to speed it up."

I once got a memo that referred to "our previous telephonic communication." How about "our last phone call"?

Jargon has many other lethal permutations but only two goals: To obscure — on purpose— your actual meaning (as in almost all legal and political writing) or else to show off and intimidate the reader (as in almost all corporate or bureaucratic writing).

Legal documents usually attempt to do both.

They *don't* want you to know what rights you've signed away or that haven't been granted. And they *do* want to impress you— and utterly cow you— with The Grandeur of The Law. And there's nothing like a run-in with a seven-syllable word to extract the living marrow out of the average American.

"Notwithstanding any and all abrogations by the hereunder licensor, the party of the second part agrees to undertake, forbear, and fulfill all fiduciary clauses."

Which means? If they shaft you, you still owe them money.

Political writing, too, is advanced Jargonese. And again, for a reason.

"Revenue enhancement" goes down a lot better than "we're raising your taxes." A "health promotion" bill sounds acceptably warm and fuzzy till you learn it's a ban on steak.

Professional, academic and bureaucratic jargon just nakedly wants to impress you; to take something simple that any fool would know and to try to make it sound very specialized and learned. This is the kind of writing that clamors for Respect, while it's sticking out its tongue and going, "Nyah-nyah-nyah. I'm an expert and you're not."

So the Board of Education writes a bulletin to teachers that no-kidding goes:

"When the teacher enters the facilitating mode in privatized, direct interfacing situations, a less formalistic approach will be required."

Means? If you're counseling a kid after school, don't act like a stiff.

But meanwhile, also, in its efforts to be fancy, it misuses "privatized" as well as "formalistic." (Doubt me? Look it up.)

Inside Baseball is, on occasion, an acceptable use of jargon among those who play the game. You'd rather have the doctor yelling "stat!" at the nurse when you'll be dead in twenty seconds if she doesn't "do it right this instant, if you please," but it isn't very helpful in conversing beyond the field. When you're writing for the general reader, spell it out.

Finally (I beg you) avoid the fad-of-the-week. Language, like hemlines and haircuts, has its fads, and this week's "gravitas," "parameters" and "schemas" are next week's leisure suits and polyester wigs. And while you're about avoiding things, avoid dull clichés, but please (I beg you) don't "avoid them like the plague."

RULE #5: USE WORDS THAT PAINT PICTURES

Let's suppose that we're all characters in a newspaper comic strip—which possibly we are. Everyone's got a couple of bubbles over his head: a scalloped Thought Bubble and a smooth Speech Bubble.

If I were speaking right now, my Speech Bubble would fill with the exact words I said, and my Thought Bubble would fill with... a picture of a person with a Thought Bubble and a Speech Bubble hanging over his head, since that's the image that I just now painted with my words.

Further, as I speak— if my words have been exact (clear, concrete)— the Thought Bubble over *your* head has filled with the same image. Or approximately the same.

We'll never know for sure.

Just as we'll never know that when *I* say, "The werewolf was wearing a red shirt," that each of us is seeing the exact same werewolf, let alone the same wine-colored Ralph Lauren shirt.

The ongoing point is that nobody ever knows what's in somebody else's bubble. We attempt, through language, to create a synchronous thought, but our language, at its best, is a highly approximate tool. But when it *isn't* at its best, it isn't anything but noise.

My Goal, When I Speak, Is To Transfer The Images From *My* Thought Bubble To *Your* Thought Bubble As Exactly As I Can.

I had a hamburger for lunch.

I had a tasteless overcooked hamburger for lunch.

I had a fat juicy hamburger smothered in sautéed onions on thick, lightly toasted sourdough garlic bread, served on a silver platter.

You begin to see pictures. You are possibly getting hungry. Which is why even radio advertising works.

Carefully chosen words can paint three-dimensional pictures in somebody else's mind, so the point is, first, to pick the words that can do it. With the power to do it. To make *me* see what *you* see. (Or taste it; or feel it. Or mentally grasp your concept.)

The second point that maybe comes out of my written lunch is that the best— or, at any rate, the fastest— way to do it (as a general rule) is with concrete— and therefore, picturable— images. *Sensual* images. With concrete but cannily selected detail.

Pay attention to this statement:

In the period from the 1930's to the 1990's, the patterns of wealth distribution in America changed. From a country with a few rich and many poor, to a country that appeared to be predominantly middle class, to a country where the middle class was getting thinned, and many more were getting rich and many more were getting poor.

There's nothing wrong with that statement. I believe that it's clear. But it's immediately clearer if I tell you that:

In other words, the pattern of wealth distribution in America seemed to go from a pyramid ... to a diamond... to an hourglass.

Bingo! You see it. I took the abstract and I made it concrete. Not only can you see it, but because you can see it, you're more likely to remember it. When you try to recall it, you can call back the *image*. Thoughts that are visual are easier to get.

That's why "I see" comes to mean "I understand."

When you write, try to write as concretely as you can. Again, with common sense. You don't have to rebus everything you write.

RULE #6:
ANALOGIES, METAPHORS AND SIMILES ARE PAINT.

That example of economic imagery above was— technically speaking— a form of analogy.

When you make an analogy, you're implying a similarity between two different things in order to clarify one of the two things. Analogies are, therefore, generally most effective when they finger a similarity between a hazy abstraction and a concrete idea—which can then help the reader to visualize the abstraction.

A simile is just another form of analogy. It likens two essentially unlike things by joining them together with a "like" or an "as." Whenever an analogy contains *like* or *as*, you can confidently state you're in the presence of a simile. Try these, from the mystery writer Raymond Chandler:

"She looked almost as hard to get as a haircut."

"The voice dragged itself out of her throat like a sick man getting out of bed."

As quiet as a mouse is a simile too— though, let's put it this way, it's *flat as a board.*

The purpose of a simile, again, is to clarify; the best of them can light up the buttons in your head.

Finally, the metaphor: an equivalent similarity between two dissimilar things but without "like" or "as." For instance:

We're ships that pass in the night.

Clearly that isn't a literal statement. Even if we're steely and broad in the beam, you and I aren't ships. The statement is metaphorical. So is, for instance: *My heart is on fire.* Though I once had a character say in a novel, "There are no metaphors in war. When you say your heart's on fire, it probably is."

And again, George Orwell, whose hobby was language, said "metaphor assists thought by sharply evoking a visual image."

Okay. Words are tools.

You can use them as bludgeons— to pound all the life and the meaning out of your thoughts— or as flashlights that illuminate.

They can also be toys, things you can play with. As Chandler played with similes. As puns "play on words." But even an everyday noun or a verb can be enjoyably exact.

His aunt gave him a kiss.

His aunt inflicted a kiss.

Clear, exact, and a model of brevity. I didn't have to tell you in another barrage of words that the kiss wasn't welcome, or seven other things. I've already told you in one little (power-packed, wisely-chosen) word.

What we're starting to get into is a part of Step Five—the part where you effectively clarify and simplify and sharpen what you wrote. The part where you edit.

3.

EDITING YOUR PROSE (SCULPTURING YOUR SENTENCES, SHARPENING YOUR POINTS)

There are, to reiterate, four basic rules about editing your prose:

BE CLEAR, BE EXACT, BE NATURAL, BE BRIEF.

Ideally, the four of them should go hand in hand. And often, and without much effort, they do.

It was raining is unquestionably briefer, clearer, more natural and exact than:

A lot of this wet stuff was falling from the sky, or the stiff, *We were experiencing modest precipitation.*

But often, they don't. At least not in your first draft. You may really have to work to make them one-in-the-same-thing. You may even have to sweat.

It's been rumored that Kipling once wrote to his editor: "Sorry to have written you such a long letter but I didn't have the time to write you a short one." Which offers you a clue, or at least a consolation. Being brief is hard work. It takes more of *your* time to take less of your readers'.

Why bother? you may ask. Why bother sweating? What difference does it make? Answer: A big one.

Your goal, in writing, is to put your thoughts quickly and clearly into my head. Accent on "quickly."

If you're slow— if your writing seems to beat around the bush— if you squander fifty words where a single one would do— my thought bubble flashes me a long string of ZZZ's. And if you don't put me to sleep, you're going to seriously annoy me. I'm annoyed, I'll start to skim. *And I could skim right over the big point you want to make.* Or else just...stop reading.

Your goal is to keep me riveted to the page so you can tell me what you want (or what you think, or what you have).

And you'll lose me if you don't tell me naturally, exactly, clearly, and fast.

So from your point of view, it's worth working on your prose.

REFINE YOUR SENTENCES.

Chisel away the fat.

The ogre wore a sort of an angry expression could easily be pared to: *The ogre looked angry.* Not only shorter, but clearer, more direct— and you sound more confident.

You don't, however, have to chisel away the charm.

Chandler's description—*It was a blonde. A blonde to make a bishop kick a hole in a stained glass window* — can not be chiseled to *The girl was blonde.*

In 1918, William Strunk, Jr. wrote a classic little book called *The Elements of Style* (later expanded by E.B. White) in which, while touting the virtues concision, he cautioned that consise was not the same as flat or colorless or curt, but rather entailed the art of making "every word tell."

He meant "tell" in the sense of "to have an effect; to make an impact."

The irony is that every word "tells" whether you want it to or not. It talks about you behind your back and it can say nasty things. Use too many words, you can give the impression that you're stiff and a bore, or a sloppy thinker, or uncertain of your facts.

THE GENERAL ASSUMPTION IS THAT FAT PROSE COMES FROM FAT HEADS

So for openers, tighten those tired locutions:

TIRED LOCUTION	MADE TIGHT
In spite of the fact that...	*although*
Due to the fact that...	*because*
With regard to....	*about*
In the majority of instances...	*usually/ mostly*

In the event of...	*if*
Somewhere in the area of...	*approximately/about*
At the current time...	*now*
Make contact with...	*call/meet/write/email*
Do you have any specific knowledge of this matter?	*What do you know about this?*

See what you can do with the following clumps of lard. Your assignment is to pare them to the minimum number of words while retaining the pertinent facts— and to make them sound natural, absolutely clear, and devoid of either buzzwords or deadening clichés.

BAD EXAMPLE #1:

It was the consensus of our department that, considering the timeline and the ground rules that were offered by your company's creatives, a dynamic, impactful educational module cannot be successfully designed by our team. In the interests of resolving this structural roadblock, we suggest it might be helpful to interface directly with your upper eschelon in the interests of hopefully rethinking the procedures. Please let us know at your earliest convenience when a meeting such as this might be arranged to take place. (82 words)

BAD EXAMPLE #2:

The Elements of Style offers this bad example— not only a paradigm of too many words but also of a bumpy ride on a choppy sea. Your assignment: smooth the passage and also make it fast.

Macbeth was very ambitious. This led him to wish to become King of Scotland. The witches told him that this wish of his would come true. The King of Scotland at this time was Duncan. Encouraged by his wife, Macbeth murdered Duncan. He was thus enabled to succeed Duncan as king. (51 words.)

And remember to apply each of the four rules, and all at the same time. Be clear, be exact, be natural, be brief. (Possible solutions at the end of this chapter.)

Since the best way to teach yourself the fine art of brevity is to practice being brief, more practice can only help. Even better, it might surprise you with a truly astonishing fact: that brevity *aids* clarity. So—try again.

Here's another thing to try.

You've got a $50 assignment from The Movie Encyclopedia to deliver the gist of a movie in 60 words max, with a 5-buck-a-word bonus for every word under the 60. On the other hand, if your entry isn't utterly smooth and clear, if it doesn't convey the essence, then it doesn't get published at all, and you unfortunately earn zilch.

Try it, using, let's say, *The Wizard of Oz* and *Jaws*, though you can substitute what you will. (And again, suggested entries will appear in the course of time.)

Finally, try this: 700 words on your professional experience. If you're lacking in it, try your educational experience and your extracurricular kicks. Done? Cut it in half. Done? Halve it again. Done? Halve it again. You've just completed the first big step towards a good resumé. You've focussed on what's important.

There are moments, however, when the four big Have To's are at war with each other. When you have to make a choice. When it's impossible to be both brief and exact (or exact and clear) and you simply have to sacrifice one for another.

**IN NONFICTION WRITING,
THERE IS NEVER AN EXCUSE TO SACRIFICE CLARITY.**

If you were playing a chess game, clarity's your king; it's the point of the whole game and it must be protected at all other costs. (Though remember: your goal is to sacrifice nothing, surrender no pieces, hold on to all four. So please don't be lazy. Try, try again.)

**PROBLEM #1:
YOU MAY HAVE TO CHOOSE BETWEEN EXACT AND BRIEF.**

For example:

A truck.

A green Ford pickup.

A muddy, pistachio-green Ford pickup with Louisiana plates and a dented right fender.

Please keep in mind that this truck is symbolic. It can stand for an object, an act, an idea— or anything you write about.

The question at hand is: which should you sacrifice— exactness or speed? Answer: it depends.

"When I got to the office, a truck was parked in my usual spot."

"My father just bought me a green Ford pickup."

"Listen, Officer, the shotgun was fired from a muddy, pistachio-green Ford pickup with Louisiana plates and a dented right fender."

First case, you'll give up exactly for fast. The exact kind of truck is completely irrelevant. The point you want to make is: you lost your parking space. Which is possibly a part of your reason for being late. Which was actually your point.

Second case, you'll want to tell me what kind of truck. If you don't, I'll have to ask. ("Oh yeah? What kind?")

However, if it happens that the truck your father bought you was banged-up and ancient, that's a lot more important than the color or the make. So in the interests of brevity, you'll tell me what's important and *only* what's important:

"My father bought me a half-wrecked, rusted-out '78 pickup."

Third case, you'll sacrifice brevity for detail. A sniper's on the loose and you want to see him caught.

But now, turn it around.

"When I got to the office, a muddy pistachio-green Ford pickup with Louisiana plates and a dented right fender was sitting in my spot."

As your reader, I now expect your truck to be important. Otherwise, why are you bothering me about it? I expect Donald Trump to step out of that truck. Or I expect it to explode.

If not, you've misled me. And not only that, you've distracted and confused me. You've begun to plow ahead— you're continuing your story— only *I'm* going, "Wait a second! What about the truck?" And pretty soon I get angry: Why have you forced me to imagine this entirely irrelevant truck? If you want me to follow you, why are you purposely cluttering the highway with a (stalled, muddy, dented, pistachio-green) truck?

A Truck Can Be Anything That Isn't Immediately (Or Eventually) Useful. A Truck Is Irrelevance.

"I'm sorry I missed the meeting. I was in the hospital with pneumonia."

"I'm sorry I missed the meeting. I'd been having a fever for a couple of days and a sort of a bad cough and I thought it was just a cold but then finally on Saturday I went to see the doctor and he said it was pneumonia and I wound up in the hospital."

Your fever is a truck. Your cough is a truck. Your delay in visiting your doctor is a truck. It's irrelevant detail. It's the answer to the wrong question. It's the answer to: "What are the symptoms of pneumonia?" Or "How come it took you so long to know you had it?" It's *not* the answer to: "Why did you miss the meeting?"

Put All Your Energy Towards Making Your Point And Use Details Only To Clarify Your Point.

I'm not retracting my advice that you ask yourself the five news questions. I'm stressing my advice that you answer them only when your reader might reasonably and sensibly ask them. Otherwise, they're trucks,

Watch out for trucks. They come in many varieties. If your paragraph is discussing the budget for your movie, don't suddenly hit me with a riff about the plot. Your plot is a truck. Drive it into another paragraph or out of the whole picture.

Ask Yourself Of Absolutely Everything You Write:
Is This A Truck?

Problem #2:
You May Have To Choose Between Exact And Clear.

I could say, with relative confidence to most of you reading this: "The waiter looked exactly like Bill Clinton." Brief, clear, exact, and there's a picture in your head— if you can picture Bill Clinton.

My writing that presumes that the majority of my readers can picture Bill Clinton, and if 5% can't, I can choose to sacrifice *their* understanding for the sake of the greater— more exact— understanding of everybody else. Or at least make a reasonable case that I could.

But try something else: "The waiter looked exactly like Jean-Paul Belmondo." Thud. Or 97½% thud. In my efforts to be exact, I've been stunningly unclear. And though a couple of aging fans of the French *Nouvelle Vague* might be gurgling with delight (which is cool if I'm writing for the *Cahiers du Cinema*), the rest of the world is blank. As many of you were when I dragged in the *Nouvelle Vague* (which is French for *The New Wave*, a term used to describe the French films of the 1960's which were written about in the arty *Cahiers du Cinema*— or *Notebook About the Movies*— and one of whose shining stars was...the guy who looked like the waiter). Which seamlessly gets us into—

PROBLEM #3:
YOU MAY HAVE TO CHOOSE BETWEEN BRIEF AND CLEAR.

Just think, for a moment, about the trouble I might have saved— for everybody concerned— if I'd traded being "exact" for straightforwardly being "clear" and just clearly described the waiter who looked like the French star. But once I started babbling about waves and *cahiers*, I simply had to define my terms. And though I tried to do it tersely, I still had to spend the words.

The same principle applies when you're explaining something otherwise technical and arcane to a broad general audience. No matter how exact your terminology might be, how immediately clear it is to people in your field, you can't instruct your readership to puffledrate the stanifram if you haven't first told them what a stanifram is and exactly where to find it, and additionally explained the full procedure of puffledration. Don't use acronyms before you've spelled them out. Or any "terms of the art" if you haven't defined them first. Otherwise, it's not only jargon, it's deep fog.

To repeat it, the point's this:

Never, *ever* sacrifice clarity, not even for exactness. Sub-point:

What's "clear" may vary with your readers. Always (always!) keep your audience in mind.

PROBLEM #4:
YOU MAY HAVE TO CHOOSE BETWEEN NATURAL AND CLEAR.

(Though it's hard to imagine when, and even harder to think of why.) There's a way to sound natural on even the most trying and formidable occasions. It's a subtle matter of tone. A note to the cat sitter is different, in tone, from a sympathy letter to a casual acquaintance, or a letter to a stranger who's inquired about your wares. But don't let the context get you into a frozen knot. Being natural has degrees, and *I was so very sorry to hear about Jonah's death* is the natural, direct and personal way of saying *Deepest sympathies at your loss.*

An occasion may arise when humanity and clarity have suddenly gone to war, and the ultimate solution is to hide behind quotes, wherein you get to blame the turgidity on its source. Then, too, there's the scare-quote—an impudent use of quotation marks that allows you to sound turgid in the interest of being exact while conveying a "hey, listen folks, that didn't come outta *me*" and "I think it's absurd, too."

The memo spelled out how to "interface with students," to "puffledrate stani-frams" and "impactfully" and "hopefully" alter the way we work.

Scare-quotes can also indicate irony (*The "experts" had the answers*) or encompass a dubious premise (*The "vast right wing conspiracy" had apparently eaten her homework*) or a carefully used cliché. (*"The devil made me do it" is not a legal excuse.*)

Following these rules when you're editing your work will "result in a win-win" for both you and your readers.

There's more, of course, to editing than simply defatting, there's also dekinking, and the kinkiest sentences involve the unnatural use of the Passive Voice.

STIFLE THE PASSIVE VOICE.

Let's first define terms. That vaunted example of textbook-perfect prose, The Complete Sentence, has a subject and a verb and, if necessary, an object. (Skip to Chapter 5 if I've left you scratching your head.) A conventional sentence— a sentence that's written in what's known as the Active Voice— will proceed in that order: subject, verb, object (actor, act, acted on). As:

I hit John.

The horse dragged the cart.

Whoever's doing the action is the subject of the sentence.

The passive voice, however, puts the cart before the horse. Specifically, it turns the object of the action into the subject of the sentence.

John was hit by me.

The cart was dragged by the horse.

Poor passive John (who just stood there getting hit) is now the subject of the sentence. It's an awkward sentence, at that, and one you'd rarely ever speak so why on earth would you ever write it? In addition to sounding silly, the actor now appears to be wriggling off the hook, not quite being man enough to squarely admit "I did it." Even the horse appears to be shy. And in any case, the twisted contortions of passivity are painful to behold.

The plane was gotten onto by too many people.

The poetry was being read by its poet.

Business writing, alas, is a birthing room of passivity in which nobody's ever wrong but where passive "mistakes were made," and where nobody's recommending, suspecting, or opining, as in "*It* is recommended" or "*It* was generally thought." Business writers fall into endless wells of passivity as a way to cover their tails, or because, for obscure reasons, they presume that it's appropriately modest and refined. In fact, it's syntactic torture; and not only that, it's dehumanized and lame.

Extra hours are being worked in order to meet the deadline.

The sentence, as written there, is leached of its flesh and blood. The hours (the subject) are apparently being worked by those mysterious elfin forces who arrive, at the crack of dawn, to take the car keys out of your pocket and the glasses off of your desk. Try, *People are working overtime... The staff recommends...* and even, though it hurts a bit, *Oops. We made a mistake.*

Yes, there are times when passivity is apt. When the object of the action is really and truly the subject of the sentence by virtue of the fact that it's the subject under discussion.

Granny's nut shop was invaded by a couple of rabid squirrels.

The Picasso mural was ruined by the fire.

Structuring sentences to make them bend to your will is another refinement of editing, which leads to another point.

JUST AS JOKES SHOULD HAVE PUNCH LINES, INDIVIDUAL SENTENCES SHOULD HAVE PUNCH *WORDS*.

And to illustrate that one, I'll invert the last sentence: Individual sentences should have punch words, just as jokes should have punch lines. See? Falls apart. Isn't nearly as punchy, isn't nearly as clear. The point of it was shyly embedded in the middle, and the point is, you want to end your sentence with... the point. Or with the unexpected element. The emphasis. The twist.

Ask yourself: Would Thomas Hobbes have made *Bartlett's* had he reckoned the life of man to be "short, brutal and nasty" instead of "nasty, brutal and short"? And if Hamlet had merely yammered that "The soul of wit is brevity," or that ultimately "The question is To be or not To be," would you have had to read him in high school?

ORGANIZE YOUR SENTENCES SO YOUR POINT IS NEVER BURIED.

And since "buried," or so I thought, was the most important word in the line, I specifically didn't put it "so you never bury your point."

Similarly, attempt to organize your paragraphs. Ideally, a new paragraph should start with a new point, or at least with a new angle. Ideally, too, the paragraph should end by driving it home.

SENTENCES NEED A STRUCTURE.

Just as your overall opus needs a structure, so too your sentences. Endow them with grammatical and logical consistence; keep them tidy and of a piece.

Messy: *The book had chapters on grammar, punctuation, and telling you the ways to compose an essay.*

Neat: *The book had chapters on grammar, punctuation, and composition.*

Messy: *They used to tell us to eat a lot of protein, but now a low protein diet is preferred.*

Neat: *They used to tell us to eat a lot of protein; now they tell us not to.*

Messy: *The living room was painted, and then they papered the den.*

Neat: *They painted the living room, and then papered the den.*

The neat ones are known as "parallel constructions." You, can, with little effort, figure out why, and then edit your work accordingly.

The Complete Vs The Incomplete Sentence.

I confess to a major sin. I frequently break the rule about incomplete sentences and how you should never write them. But then, as I said before, it's important to at least know the rules that you plan to break. So you'll know why you're breaking them. There. I did it again. "So you'll know why you're breaking them" is not a complete sentence. Let's define a complete sentence: It's got a subject and a verb (and, if necessary, an object). It does not begin with a *so*, and it does not begin with a *which*. Which is frequently inconvenient (see? I did it again) since a sentence beginning with either has advantages all of its own. Emphasis, for one thing. Rhythm, for quite another. (*And I did it twice in a row!*)

But here's why the rule exists:

The cyanide filled the room. Which was small and overcrowded.

I wanted to go to school. Because I wanted a better job.

I met her in Madrid. A contessa, or so she said, with a small pet cockatoo and a son with a roving eye.

Though the latter doesn't offend me, neither would putting it right by creating a single sentence, with a dash or a comma after the word *Madrid*. But the other two are atrocious, and no redeeming reason can be found for the *faux pas*.

No Sentence Is An Island.

Think of your sentences as part of a larger team. The team is the paragraph. (The paragraph is part of a team called the page; and the page, of the chapter; and the chapter, of the book. But let's leave that alone for now.)

The point is, your sentences lean on the ones before them, and lead to the ones that follow. And they all have to get along. This is partly a matter of rhythm (a subject that's coming up) and then partly a matter of balance. Your goal is to make them flow. To move, so smoothly, from one line to the next, that your reader is never jostled, never stumbles and hits a rock.

In the phase where you're editing, read what you've written straight through in a single gulp. Wherever your eye stumbles, rewrite it to make it smooth.

Keep in mind, too, that to keep your reader awake, you'll want to vary the kinds of sentences you use in a block of text— to attack them in different ways. And there are, indeed, infinite ways to attack a sentence. All it takes is a little thought:

After sobbing a long while, he stopped, and ate his prunes.
He sobbed for a long while, then stopped and ate his prunes.
After a long while, he stopped sobbing and ate his prunes.
After he stopped sobbing, he finally ate the prunes.
He sobbed and sobbed, but in the end, ate his prunes.
He finally ate his prunes, but not before putting on a long show of sobbing.
He did eat the prunes, but only after sobbing for the better part of an hour.

He sobbed. The depths of his anguish surprised him. It was, after all, only a plate of prunes. His sister had told him it was dead waterbugs, drowned in the bathtub and floating in toxic rust. But why would his mother feed him dead rusty bugs? Surely, she adored him, if only a little bit. And didn't he, finally, owe her the gift of trust? He fought back his hesitance. He ate them. And died.

That last, by the way, was specifically meant to illustrate how varying the structure of your serial sentences, one against the other, keeps a paragraph alive. You can analyze it at leisure. (And then, eat your prunes!)

POSSIBLE SOLUTIONS TO THE EDITING ASSIGNMENTS:

Here's the awful original:

It was the consensus of our department that, considering the timeline and the ground rules that were offered by your company's creatives, a dynamic, impactful educational module cannot be successfully designed by our team. In the interests of resolving this structural roadblock, we suggest it might be helpful to interface directly with your upper eschelon in the interests of hopefully rethinking the procedures. Please let us know at your earliest convenience when a meeting such as this could be arranged to take place. (82 words)

Here's a possible revision:

We think we can do a better job for you if we can change some of the guidelines. We'd like to meet with your creative directors to discuss our concerns and will call you tomorrow to arrange an appointment. (39 words)

Here's the second awful original— whose rhythm can drive you mad—

Macbeth was very ambitious. This led him to wish to become King of Scotland. The witches told him that this wish of his would come true. The King of Scotland at this time was Duncan. Encouraged by his wife, Macbeth murdered Duncan. He was thus enabled to succeed Duncan as king. (51 words.)

Okay, how's this?

Driven by the prophesy of the witches and the goading of his wife, Macbeth killed Duncan and succeeded him to the Scottish throne. (27 words)

But wait. That version deleted his ambition. Okay, try again.

The flame of Macbeth's ambition was ignited by the witches and fanned by his wife; he wanted to be king and killed to get his wish. (26 words)

Okay. A little smoother but, hey, king of what? not to mention killed whom? And then what did the witches *do*?

Let's try again.

Macbeth, made bold by the prophesy of the witches, the goading of his wife, and his own hot ambitions, killed Duncan, King of Scotland, and replaced him on the throne. (30 words.)

Clear, natural, brief and exact (hitting all the bases— ambition, wife, witches, prophesy, murder, Duncan, Scotland, king).

The point is: it's work. And the point is, it's worth it. And the point is, there's more than one way to defat a cat.

The Elements of Style offers a different resolution (and for that, buy the book):

About those movies.

My own quick take on *The Wizard of Oz* was this:

A hurricane hurtles a girl from Kansas to adventures in the mythical kingdom of Oz where she learns about friendship, magic and danger, and the ultimate lesson that "there's no place like home." (33 words)

Leonard Maltin, in "TV Movies" (1982) did it like this: *American classic of Kansas girl sailing "over the rainbow" to the land of Oz with assorted unusual friends.* (18 words)

And "Hallowell's Film and Video Guide" (1999) had yet another angle: *Unhappy Dorothy runs away from home, has adventures in a fantasy land, but finally decides that happiness was in her own backyard all the time.* (25 words)

For *Jaws*, Leonard Maltin had 38 words:

New England shore community is terrorized by shark attacks; local cop, ichthyologist and salty shark expert determine to kill the attacker. A rare case of a bubble gum story scoring as a terrific movie. Hold onto your seats! (38 words)

Hallowell's did it in 10:

A man-eating shark causes havoc off the Long Island coast.

I myself took a different, more "film critic" angle, coming in at 36 (or 51) words:

Greed and adventure on the coast of Long Island as two sets of sharks (the resort-town merchants and the snaggle-toothed fish) imperil the tourists. The ending is a slam-bang, bone-chilling shark hunt (36) *as a cop, a scientist, and a seasoned shark hunter take to the high seas.* (51)

I'm still, in fact, wondering whether adding those fifteen ultimate words was worth losing the extra money the newspaper promised, but I'll leave it to you to decide.

We've now entered the realm in which the hard task of editing confronts you with hard choices— a sacrifice of words and occasionally of facts— a decision to be made on a need-to-know basis. (Does the reader need to know at this particular time that the king's name was Duncan, that the girl's name was Dorothy, that greed was part of the plot, or even that the hunters had various occupations? If you also had the luxury of a longer piece of prose, could you tell me this later? Should you have told me this before? Should you tell me this at all? In complex passages where something's gotta go, you have to decide what. What's important; what's a truck.)

The same thing applies to your autobiography. What's important in the sales pitch to sell yourself for a job? For that particular job? And what— a Mercedes or not— is a truck?

4.

TONE, RHYTHM, AND PUNCTUATION

Yes, there are textbook rules about punctuation, but it's not my intention to deal with them all here (though I'll deal with them a little and refer you to a grammar book to flummox you with the rest). My intention is to offer an alternative school of thought, a do-it-yourself version, or at least what to do when the textbook isn't around.

Let's go back to the basic premise: If writing is like talking, and if reading is like listening and repeating the writer's words, then when you read what you've written, you can, just by listening, punctuate "by ear"— and I do literally mean that you can *hear* punctuation—that your every tittle and comma has a plangent voice of its own. Punctuation, then, is an art quite as much as it is a science— in fact, a dramatic art, since it helps or impedes meaning by affecting rhythm and tone.

Start with a simple fact: When words stick to paper, they don't make a sound. Their little mouths are taped shut. And the only voice that speaks them is the reader's inner voice, which is attempting to imitate the writer's inner voice.

Think, for a moment, about the process of reading— break it down into steps. The eye takes a gander at a bunch of visual symbols; the mind then immediately translates them into sounds, the sounds that comprise words. And the mind actually "says" them — hollers them, whispers them, whatever appears right— but very definitely says them. It also takes in, and similarly translates, the symbols of punctuation, and pronounces them too. Reading rapidly, you're not too aware of what you're doing (though you are when you're reading slowly, or reading out loud) but it happens in either case. Your inner voice chatters and jabbers when you read, taking audio directions from the symbols on the page. Silent, but desperately gesturing symbols.

And they have to be clear. Like hand signals in a football game, they're calling the whole play. And with all that in mind, let's talk about tone—and, to start with:

TONE OF VOICE.

Try this one:

"Get outta here."

The words on the page are just lying there inert— silent, toneless, and to that extent, ambiguous. What they mean—or what the reader interprets them to mean— what he decides that *you meant*— depends on how he says them.

"Get outta here!!" (Terminal and threatening anger.)
"Get outta here." (A prudent warning to a friend)
"Aw, get outta here." (Listen, Charlie, don't put me on.)

The tone that it's spoken in can make all the difference. But the tone, when it's written isn't up to the writer, it's up to the reader, to the reader's inner voice. Which has to be carefully directed by the writer. (Sarcasm, thus, can fall dangerously flat or be dangerously misconstrued if it's carelessly directed.)

So how can you make that difference come across?

Sometimes you do it with a well-constructed context, surrounding things with helpful unambiguous words or phrases. (Like the "aw" up above.)

Sometimes you do it with simple punctuation. Write it in italics, follow it with an exclam.

Sometimes— but only if you're very, very skillful— you can do it with ryhthm.

And sometimes it's simply impossible to do. You have to reword it. Nor is it only jokes that can get you into trouble. Factual phrases, too, can be totally misread.

They didn't do it well however they did it.
They didn't do it well; however, they did it.

The first version tells us that no matter how they did it, they totally screwed it up and you're mightily displeased. The second version says that while they didn't do it well, they at least did do it and you're somewhat appeased.

You accomplished that absolutely major difference in meaning through a sprinkle of punctuation.

Two points arise. First, that you have to learn what punctuation means— to the written sentence, and then to the reader's ear— and second, that you always have to write to the reader's ear.

Yet another good reason to test drive your sentences— in this case, to hand your manuscript to a friend and have him read it to himself either silently or aloud. Where ambiguity is possible, you can't trust yourself because your own inner voice is entirely biased. You know what you meant to say and the way you meant to say it, so that's how you'll hear it and that's how you'll read it. But what your reader will do with it, heaven only knows.

Okay, we've just talked about one kind of tone, but tone, like a cat, has a lot of different lives.

For instance, you can talk about the tone of a word in the same way you'd talk about tone in music. Literally, the pitch— the note that it's said on. Is it A or B flat? And further, do you say it in a short choppy chord or a long suspended Seventh?

In Mandarin Chinese— a very musical language— the pitch affects the meaning. If you say the word *bao* in a high soprano pitch, then the word means *mother;* say it low, it means *house.* But the notion that pitch can be a hard clue to meaning isn't totally foreign.

Listen carefully to the difference:

You went there. Didn't you.

You went there, didn't you?

The exact same words, and again, different meanings.

The first one, to me, is pretty much an accusation. Someone accusing someone of going into the attic *where I told you not to go.* The second one's an absolutely innocent question. The "there" could be Yosemite Park or the Taj Mahal.

And once again, the difference was accomplished through punctuation which affected, in this case, both the rhythm and the pitch. The period instructed you to pause and lower your voice, and the question mark, to raise it. The first tone is heavy; the second one is light.

Thus, I introduce you to my simple but heretical view of punctuation:

PUNCTUATION IS A STAGE DIRECTION FOR THE EYE AND FOR THE READER'S INNER VOICE.

Let's start with the standard symbols: what they mean to the written sentence, what they mean to inner voice.

Throughout, I've been talking about prose in the terms of music. Tone. Rhythm. Pitch. This is not accidental. The spoken sentence is a lot like the musical phrase. Therefore it follows that the written sentence is somewhat analogous to the sheet music line. In addition to printing notes (the equivalent of words), it also includes the rests— the *pauses* between the words. And not only do the symbols instruct you where to pause, they also tell you for how long. Full beat; half-beat; quarter-beat, etc. And without that rhythm— and without the written symbols for quantifying rhythm— there would be no music. No musical logic. No rhythm; no rhyme.

Punctuation marks, then, are like musical rests. And with that much in mind, let's explore them and what they mean.

(.) **THE PERIOD** usually means a one-beat pause. End of a statement. As for tone, your voice drops on the word before the dot or at least stays level. In grammatical terms, it means the end of what's known as a "complete sentence," defined by the book as a collection of words that has a subject (a noun) and a predicate (a verb and any burden the verb carries).

The princess slept.

The princess was sleeping very soundly on the pea.

The underlined phrases constitute the predicate.

A period is a symbol that informs your alert reader that, miraculously, a complete sentence has been completed. Therefore, before you put a period on a page, look over the words before it. If they include the requisite members, you can finish them off with a dot. (See my previous Confession at the end of Chapter 3.)

(,) **THE COMMA** is a half- or a quarter-beat pause. A slight hesitation. A comma clears the air between clauses within a sentence or the items on a list. When you're heading for a comma, your voice takes a pause but your pitch doesn't drop, thus allowing the implication that the thought is "to be continued." Those commas that indicate a pause and hold-pitch *and really mean what they're saying* are user-friendly. They help guide the reader through a thorny thicket in which he might otherwise tend to get lost. And while the lack of such commas can endanger your meaning, so can a comma that's tossed in the wrong spot— either through sloppiness or mindless adherence to obstructive grammatical rules, i.e., the intrusion of the "silent comma," more on which later.

AS A GENERAL RULE, WHILE A COMMA IS A PAUSE, ITS ABSENCE IS A NICE GREEN LIGHT FOR THE READER'S EYE, TELLING HIM TO KEEP ON PLOWING RIGHT AHEAD.

So with every sentence you write, listen hard to your own voice. If you need a slight pause (or a visual separation) you do need a comma. If you don't, you don't.

(I couldn't write the sentence *If you don't, you don't* without a comma in the middle.)

For a few more examples: *You're doing it right* is vastly different from *You're doing it, right?* Or play around with these, and pay attention to your voice;

Overnight, plane fares rose 10%.

Overnight plane fares rose 10%.

In the first case, the fares rose abruptly on all flights; in the second, the fares rose on night flights only. In the first case, you paused on account of the comma, and the meaning, as the writer intended, became clear.

Try this one:

The woman, with improbable self-importance, was lecturing on poetics.

The woman with improbable self-importance was lecturing on poetics.

Again, both the meaning and the recitation differ. The first means the woman was lecturing self-importantly. The next, that the improbably self-important woman (as opposed to the six other women in the room) was the one who was yakking. If you listen to yourself as you silently say the sentence, you'll hear where you need the pause, and then write it accordingly.

Have faith; you've got a comma barometer in your ear.

The Silent Comma

This is the one I hate. It follows the textbooks and screws up the sentence, causing the eye to stumble and the reading to go awry. This, for example:

He claims to have experience, but, in fact, it's irrelevant, since, as you know, we need someone who speaks English.

I repeat, that's correct. But it's utterly unreadable. If you want to stay correct, you'll either have to rewrite it (*His experience is irrelevant since he doesn't speak English*) or... play it by ear. Listen to where you pause and place your commas accordingly, fervently keeping in mind that you're writing to communicate, not simply to get an A in Ms. O'Shaugnessy's seventh grade.

The Misuse Of Commas

Of all punctuation marks, the comma is most abused. It's used where it shouldn't be, and shouldn't be where it's used.

It shouldn't be used to link two complete sentences.

I sent the letter, I jumped.

Confusion sets in. What, one may wonder, has one to do with the other? By linking the two with a comma, I've implied they're connected by some form of logic, since the reader's wary assumption is that everything done in ink between the initial capital letter and the final ebony dot is all part of the same thought. What I need to restore sanity is a period or a connective— a word that explains how (in what way) the clauses are linked.

I sent the letter <u>and</u> <u>then</u> I jumped.

And while I'm not exactly sure what that would mean in the real world (except possibly the answer to *Tell me, did you mail your suicide note before or after you jumped from the bridge?*) at any rate, grammatically, it's now a complete thought.

Similar distraction is provided when you marry two sentences in haste:

The suffragette furiously pounded on the door, it was answered by the misogynist.

Clearly, these two should have never gotten together. They need to be separated at least by a period or, perhaps even better in this particular instance, by the glorious semi-colon.

The suffragette furiously pounded on the door; it was answered by the misogynist.

Allow me to explain:

Anything that's worthy of the title Complete Sentence is also known familiarly as an independent clause. It's acceptable to merge two independent clauses, either with a connective (as we did with *and then*) or whenever the two clauses are implicitly connected. What usually connects them (in the intellectual sense) is a tacit assumption of cause or consequence, of simultaneity, of parallel construction, or of further explanation, and that's where the semi-colon enters our little tale— smack between the two clauses.

(;) **THE SEMI-COLON** is a ¾ pause. Shorter than a period but longer than a comma. The reader's eye pauses briefly for a comma but the barrier's low; he can jump right over it and faster than you'd like. But when a semi-colon comes, he bumps against a wall; has to stop; drive around. A semi-colon is not interchangeable with a comma. A semi-colon implies an intimate relationship between two notions (the thoughts on either side) but nonetheless allows them to maintain their independence. Like living together but not getting married.

It was snowing; the planes couldn't land on the field.
He was desperate for her to believe him; she could see it in his eyes.
The shots rang out. She screamed; I ducked.
The report was due on the seventh; we finished it on the tenth.
For a nonagenarian, he wasn't bad looking; he was simply too poor.

Note the relationship between the two clauses: cause and effect, parallel construction, simultaneous action, or further amplification. And sometimes—like the last two examples given above— the semi-colon itself adds a wry twist of irony (or an extracurricular meaning) by connecting the two thoughts. This subtext, indeed, is what makes it especially lovely, but even with lovely things, there's a reason to use restraint. Caution:

Don't Be Promiscuous With Semi-Colons

They're sophisticated and subtle and a kind of acquired taste. Like Russian caviar or green olives, they are not meant to substitute for peanut butter and jam. When in doubt, use a period.

Semi-Colons In Lists

There's only one place where the textbook grammarian will whack you over the knuckles if a semi-colon is lost, because its absence destroys meaning, making soup out of solid thought. When the individual items in a longer series or list simply scream for their own commas, you can only set them apart by injecting a different squiggle, and the semi-colon is it.

The members of the traveling circus took a bow: Krapotkin, the tamer, Melissa, the lion, the two-headed leprechaun, Larry and Louise.

Quick now: How many troupers took a bow? 3? 4? 7? 6? And if four, who's the tamer?

The members of the traveling circus took a bow: Krapotkin, the tamer; Melissa, the lion; the two-headed leprechaun, Larry and Louise. (Answer: 3)

Or you can play around with this:

The panel consisted of: the former Vice President, Sheraton Welles, an alumnus of Harvard, Jefferson Spite, the head of Consolidated Limited, Inc., a sponsor of the conference, and the night's honoree.

Aside from "how many?" the questions grow thick. Like... who went to Harvard—Mr. Spite or Mr. Welles? Is Consolidated, Spite, or neither the sponsor? And is Spite, or is somebody else, the honoree? How bewildering. Only the semi-colon knows.

(:) **<u>The Colon</u>** — a beat long—is "a mark of anticipation." The word before the colon often sounds like "ta-da!" It promises a payoff of breathtaking splendor, and summarily endows you with a chance to bate your breath.

And the prizes tonight are: a dining set by Levitz! a weekend in Pasadena!

an electric tomato! a genuine purple cow!

Obviously, the colon isn't always so exciting. A colon can follow a word that introduces the following things: a related series of items, an example or explanation, a definition or a result, or a dramatic form of quotation.

It can follow or, better still, take the place of extraneous phrases: *For example, As follows, The point is, The result was,* and even *Therefore* and *Like this.*

Or to offer a few examples:

Talk about diversity: the movie includes an overdose of yammering mynah birds, tap dancing teddy bears, and even a reluctantly whistling kettle.

Plagued for many years with a distinct absence of joy, she tried Positive Thinking, marathon running, and eventually lobotomy: instant success.

There are many ways to resolve it: shooting, slashing, burning or divorce.

Or as he once famously put it: "Truth is the first casualty of war."

( ) **THE PARENTHESIS** is a beat but it's more than merely a beat; it sets the tone of the reader's voice. It instructs him that the parenthetical phrase is just an aside, and to kindly treat it as such. The reader will take a pause, drop his voice or read it in haste. Parentheses, in fact, are the opposite of italics.

A parenthetical phrase can also be employed for a minor elaboration:

In the Watergate incident (1974) Nixon blew his cool.

Or an incidental aside:

He phoned me (collect, from Indiana) at 10 o'clock.

Or a clarifying example:

The leading men of the '40's (Gable, Mitchum et al) had a manlier kind of appeal.

Or occasionally to set off an interjected phrase as a way of making it pop:

The stores (even the bars) were all shuttered and grimly dark.

Or where dashes have been previously used for the same purpose and you're seeking a variation. Dashes and parentheses can, in a lot of contexts, accomplish the same task. As here, for example, on page 65:

And sometimes—like the last two examples given above— the semi-colon itself adds a wry twist of irony (or an extracurricular meaning) by connecting the two thoughts.

And sometimes you can use them (or *I* do) for rhythm. More on which later.

DOES THE PERIOD GO BEFORE OR AFTER THE PARENTHESIS?

After, in the case of a parenthetical phrase that just happens to end the sentence.

He asked, "Wanna hear a joke?" (as though we could stop him).

Before, when the entire sentence is parenthetical:

He asked, "Want to hear a joke?" (At this point, Melissa summarily left the room and Sir Anthony fainted.)

(—) **THE DASH** is anything from a beat to a somewhat less-than-a-beat pause. (Shorter than parentheses but longer than a comma.) But unlike parentheses, a dash is meant to separate— and therefore call attention to— whatever's between the marks. As I previously used dashes to separate— and underscore— the point I just made. A dash says, "Pause, and give equal emphasis to what comes after." In other words, the phrase in the middle of two dashes is meant to be important, and the dashes say "Hark!"

The girl on the carpet— the girl with two heads—wore a matched pair of smiles.

There are other times, however, when one dash will do; when you simply want to separate the end of the sentence to show it's a separate but equal partner, or when you're seeking to illuminate, expand or explain, in which case the dash is more casual than a colon and less academic.

Everything frightened him—heights, open spaces, animals, traffic, and towels with initials.

At other times you'll use it for the sheer rhythmic pulse and to ensure the proper reading. "You're doing it— right?" has a slightly different nuance than "You're doing it, right?" And the difference was decided by the dash in the first example and the comma in the second.

ITALICS (*ital*) are a cue to hard-pedal, to stress the italicized word or phrase (or occasionally, syllable). Use them when you need to add urgency or emphasis. Need to, I said. Go easy on the pedal.

However, there are times when italics are the only way to make your thought clear. Take, for example, the seemingly simple sentence "She didn't love Harry."

Now say it four times, each time emphasizing a different one of the words, and you'll see that the emphasis completely changes the meaning.

She didn't love Harry. (Implies somebody else did.)
She *didn't* love Harry. (A hot denial.)
She didn't *love* Harry. (Just liked him a lot.)
She didn't love *Harry*. (She loved somebody else.)

Without italics, your sentence is ambiguous. Your reader could give it any of those meanings, so you need to tell her which.

A more quotidian use of italics has nothing to do with emphasis but simply, unemphatically, indicates titles— of books, publications, or various works of art (*The New Republic*, Plato's *Republic*, *Sex and the City*, the *Pieta*), or of transport with proper names (the *Queen Mary, Enola Gay*) or words and phrases in foreign tongues (*id est: n'est-ce pas?*) Titles—at least some of them— can also be placed in quotes.

EXCLAMATION POINTS! are used to express urgency or surprise or exceptionally strong feelings. They also usually follow a word that connotes a noise, or a marvel of revelation. When he's cued with an exclamation point, your reader duly exclaims.

Ouch! Stop! Fire! Wait! Bam! What?!! Shazam!

You can use them to say *Eureka!* You can use them to say *Aha!*; you can use them to say *They're coming! Hide in the closet! Muzzle the dog!*; you can use them to be ironic; you can use them within parentheses the way that you'd use a sic (!)[1], but I caution you— please! never! ever!— use them for minor matters. (*Oh, the oatmeal was so delicious! Meeting your mother was so much fun!!*)

1 See Chapter 6

**NO MATTER HOW YOU EMBELLISH A MOLEHILL,
IT'S NOT A MOUNTAIN OR EVEN A CHAIR.**

Be very cautious in using exclams. You're at risk of sounding hysterical or gushingly adolescent.

(?) **THE QUESTION MARK**, in spite of what the textbook writers instruct, should only be used for a genuine inquiry. *What's the climate of Northern Spain? Will you come with me to the Casbah?* or anything else you'd utter with a rising inflection. Listen to your voice. Does it rise? Use a ?. If it doesn't, then don't. Again, the examples:

You went there. Didn't you.
You went there, didn't you?

Listen to your voice. You'll hear that not everything that's worded as a question is actually a question or intended to be question. *Will you please send me the check* is hardly a bland query and should therefore end with a period (if not with an exclamation).

On the other hand, you'll hear that occasionally a sentence that's worded as a statement is actually a question and ought to be marked as such:

You're saying he's a spy?
Santa Clause is here?
Okay? Any questions? Or may we go on with the book.

("") **QUOTATION MARKS** surround the beginning and end of a passage —usually a passage that was written, spoken or scrawled in a public toilet by somebody else, and which you now want to quote verbatim— very literally, word-for-word. (Read the rulebook in Chapter 6.) Please be careful and pay attention.

The manager said that latecomers won't be admitted.

No quotation marks are required; in fact, they'd be incorrect. This is not a direct quote; this is gossip, interpretation. It's a summary; a report.

However, if he actually said it, word-for-word, and you actually want to quote him, then:

The manager said, "Latecomers won't be admitted."

That's at least the correct form (although why you'd want to bother for such a truly banal remark is a world-beating mystery). In fact, it's so banal, you could even put it like this:

The manager said latecomers won't be admitted.

But here's where we hit a curve.

According to Ms. Javonovich, only "a few elite" will be admitted after the bell.

Here, amidst your summary, you're trying to make it clear that Ms. Javonovich quite specifically uttered the damning words.

As for punctuating quotations, observe how I did it above.

A comma comes between the attribution and the quotation (i.e., *The manager said*, "...) and the period at the end comes within the enfolding marks (*...be admitted.*")

Though, of course, there's the rare exception. Like:

Who are "the few elite"?

The question here is the writer's so it's placed outside of the quotes since Ms. Javonovich wasn't asking; Ms. Javonovich seemingly *knew*.

Here's another interesting question. What about the construction when attributions come at the end? Or even in the middle? Note the commas and where they fall:

"When I use a word," Humpty Dumpty said in a rather scornful tone, "it means just what I choose it to mean—neither more nor less."

Note: that's a single sentence, interrupted by attribution. However, two sentences would be punctuated like this:

"I don't like the look of it at all," said the King. "However, it may kiss my hand, if it likes."

"I'd rather not," the cat said.

Which should answer the hanging questions. That's the model. Take it from there.

Then, too, there's the final question of using quotes marks within a quote. (When somebody says that somebody said.) This is done with a single quote mark (the apostrophe key on your board):

"No, no. Not the same thing a bit!" said the Hatter. "Why you might

just as well say that 'I see what I eat' is exactly the same thing as 'I eat what I see.' " (Note: when the sentence ends with the ', the " follows after.)

Tangentially, quotation marks, just like italics, can also be used for titles. Technically, there's a difference but it's really a minor quibble. Use one form or the other (or, in some cases, neither) but at least try to be consistent.

(The practical use of scare-quotes has been covered in Chapter 3, and the proper use of citations will be covered in Chapter 6.)

Rhythm Without The Blues.

We've talked, so far, about basic punctuation as a carrier of rhythm, and rhythm, in turn, as a carrier of meaning. But now it's time to talk about rhythm all on its own. Rhythm because it's pleasing. Rhythm because it's fun. Rhythm, in short, because. Because without it, your prose is mush. (I was just indulging in rhythm. I was doing it obviously but it's not always obvious.) Rhythm is mostly subtle. The best rhythm, in fact, can be totally undetectable but, even as it's cannily slipping under the radar, it can make all the difference between a paragraph that's pleasing and easy-to-understand, and a boring, chaotic, unfathomable mess. If everything else in your paragraph is right— if your words are exact, if your meaning and all of your implications are clear— you can still lose your reader with a flat-footed beat.

A joke isn't funny if it hasn't got the beat. Rhythm is the stuff that makes a joke funny. Or not. Comics call it timing. Writers call it rhythm, but it means the same thing. Further, rhythm is the subtext of your prose. It's the background music that's playing against your movie. It adds color. Or suspense. It can quicken your reader's pulse or it can bid him to feel serene.

It can also put him to sleep. You can hammer him into a coma with the deadly beat of a dirge, or a dumpty-dump overdose of iambic pentamenter.

A sentence with lousy rhythm can also confound your meaning by leaving your reader at sea in a sentence without ballast. Rhythm, done correctly, puts the stress on the right phrases, reinforcing your written meaning.

Four score and seven years ago,
Our fathers
Brought forth on this continent
A new nation,
Conceived in liberty
And dedicated to the proposition
That all men are created equal.

In the opening passage of the Gettysburg Address with its brilliant rhythmic attack, so perfect is Lincoln's cadence, you can lay it out like a poem, though it wasn't, of course, a poem. But hear it. Pay attention to how the rhythm carries you forth.

Four score and seven years ago... Listen to that beat. Irresistibly, the reader puts the stress on the *Four score*, each word with an equal emphasis as certain as Bang! Bang! And having done it, you've caught the rhythm that simply dances you through to the end, forcing similar equal stresses on your reading of *brought forth* and a kind of subtle parallel reading of other phrases within the line. *Seven years ago/ on this continent.* It scans, in fact, like a poem.

(/-/--) SEV-en YEARS a-go.

(/-/--) ON this CON-ti-nent.

Now all of that would be pretty but not important except for this: the rhythm bolsters the meaning. The sentence's rhythmic architecture forces the points to pop. The reader, cannily guided into pauses that bracket clauses, into forming the proper phrases, into stressing the proper words, becomes at one with the writer's thought. And that beginning of *Four score* is the magic bullet that hits the points. In *The Elements of Style,* Strunk and White, though they generally (and correctly) advise simplicity, dismiss alternative phrases— the short, more direct *Eighty-seven years ago* and the sonorous though specific *In the year of our Lord, seventeen hundred and seventy-six.* They reject them, and rightly so, and if you haven't landed on why, listen closely and read aloud.

In the year of our Lord, seventeen hundred and seventy-six, our fathers brought forth on this continent a new nation, conceived in liberty and dedicated to the proposition that all men are created equal.

See? Falls apart. Not only does it seem to go on and on and on but, without that introductory cadence of "four score," the whole sentence sags in the middle and then forces the reader's voice (perhaps through complete weariness) to throw away in a mumble the most important phrase at the end: the famous proposition that all men are created equal.

Now try it the other way:

Eighty-seven years ago, our fathers brought forth on this continent a new nation, conceived in liberty and dedicated to the proposition that all men are created equal.

Now the entire sentence seems abrupt and matter-of-fact; it's a sentence that stresses nothing, gives you nothing to stir your heart. It's as bland and as flat-out as a letter from your accountant (*Eighty-seven months ago, you bought a municipal bond*). It's a sentence, as a whole, that you'd little note nor long remember.

Rhythm becomes the key. I got. You got. Everyone's got rhythm. It's the beat of your beating blood. In fact, the way you actually talk has a rhythm. It's different for each one of us, and different perhaps in context, but it's thumping nevertheless. And writing (do I dare to repeat it?) is like talking.

In a screenplay, in the middle of a typed block of dialogue, the writer will write (*Beat*)—meaning syncopate; pause— as a guide to the actor's timing. In a novel, the writer sets the timing with punctuation or with words that contain the one and only beat that directs the line. When the novelist writes *he said*, it could be, quite straightforwardly, because the character *said*, or it could be that he needs the beats— those particular rhythmic stresses and the pattern of Da-DAH. If he needed a different rhythm— like for instance a da-da-*DAH*— then he'd give you a different rhythm: "he announced." "Raymond shrugged."

Finally, then, there's this. Rhythm has effects that go beyond its particular setting. Like the first fall of a domino, it ripples throughout the page. Change the rhythm of sentence one, and you also affect the rhythm of sentence two, three, four...and in fact, of the whole paragraph. And often the next paragraph. And the paragraph after that.

Don't believe me? Try it yourself. Pick a passage in any book, or any column, or any song that you particularly admire and make a couple of minor changes. Maybe cutting a word here, maybe adding a word there, maybe substituting a two-syllable adjective for a one. When you're done with it, start reading. Begin with the previous passage (the one that you haven't changed) and then read what you've newly wrought, and read on to whatever follows.

You'll see. About nine times in eleven, it falls apart. Easy reading becomes bumpy. What flowed becomes dammed. And the meaning or the humor or the resonance disappears.

Be conscious of easy rhythms when you're editing what you wrote. Just a little fiddling here and just a little tinkering there— even if it seems quite appropriate to the sentence— can implode the entire paragraph or even the whole work.

Whenever you've made changes, don't read them in isolation. Read the sentences— or even the paragraphs—that surround them.

5.

GRAMMAR SCHOOL
THE ELEMENTARY ELEMENTS

Yes, of *course*, you know all of this totally basic stuff. But look at it this way: it comes with the book. You've paid for it anyway, so you might as well read it. And you might be surprised.

Let's start with a few basics:

THE BASIC PARTS OF SPEECH

NOUNS, VERBS, AND GERUNDS

A NOUN is a word that refers to a person, a place or a thing. The Thing can be tangible (an apple, Samantha, Seattle, second base) or abstract (inspiration, hostility, luxury, trouble).

A noun can be the subject
or the object of a sentence.

Samantha loves trouble.

"Samantha" is the *subject* (the actor in the sentence) and "trouble" is (alas) the *object* of her affection— or to put that another way, the object of her verb.

A VERB is a word that describes an action or a state of being. "To love" is a verb, and so is "to be." (To be or not to be, that is a verb.)

There are two kinds of verbs:
Transitive and Intransitive.

A transitive verb is a form of transportation— it carries an action from a subject to an object (from a noun to a noun). It's alternatively known as an incomplete verb since it doesn't make sense when it's standing there alone:

I sent.

I completed.

Incomplete verbs lead to incomplete sentences and complete confusion. I sent...*what?* I completed...*what?* A transitive verb needs a *what* to make sense:

I sent the ransom note.

I completed the sentence.

An intransitive verb is complete in itself without further explanation: *I jumped. I sneezed.*

A GERUND is a verb that's undergone a sex change and turned into a noun. Specifically, the verb had an "ing" transplant. The suffix "ing" was added to its tail. So the verb "to dance" becomes the noun "dancing" and thus becomes a gerund. (On the other hand, not every verb that has an "ing" is automatically a gerund. The big question is: does it *function* as a noun? Does it function as the subject or the object of the act?) Better spell that one out:

Eliza is dancing. (This is "dancing" as a verb.)

Dancing is the only thing Eliza likes to do. ("Dancing" is a noun; it's the *thing* Eliza likes.)

Jack enjoys arguing. ("Arguing" is a noun.)

There's really no reason to be concerned about gerunds, or even aware of them, except when it comes to the matter of possessives. And the rule there is this:

A VERB IN NOUN'S CLOTHING
GETS TREATED LIKE A NOUN.

No matter how violent and manly the verb is, no matter what havoc it could level as a verb *(bombing, philandering)*, once it becomes a noun, it gets treated no better than a *baby* or a *dream* or any other noun. And when, as a noun, it's possessed or otherwise attributed to someone, it takes a possessive pronoun (or else a possessive noun).

Their bombing on Broadway was a blow to their egos.

My going to college didn't help me get a job.

His philandering had consequences.

Your laughing when she tripped on the carpet was bizarre.

The story about Barry's giving birth to a minotaur appeared on Page Six.

(Please see Possessives)

More About Nouns

Singulars And Plurals

Singular means one. Plural means more— in fact, it means anything from two to infinity.

About 96% of the time in English, when you're speaking of more than one, all you have to do is add an *s* to your word. But like any other rule, there are curious exceptions. ***Es*** forms the plural when the singular ends in ***s, sh, ch, x*** or ***z.*** And you can actually hear it:

*witch/the three witch**es**; lash/fifty lash**es.***

Hear the extra syllable? That's the ***e-s.***

If you can't remember the rule, just remember the extra beat. Listen closely to how it sounds:

The boxing matches
Between the foxes
Were set to waltzes,
And watched from boxes
By girls in sashes
With lowered lashes,
And boys with glasses
Who thrive on clashes.

Here's some other kinks in the rule. When the singular ends in ***y*** and the plural in ***ies***. So its:

*fair**y**/fair**ies;** dingh**y**/dingh**ies***

Or when some— but not all— of the singles that end in ***f*** become ***ves*** in the plural—like:

Of course, half a loaf is certainly better than none,
but aren't two <u>halves</u> of two <u>loaves</u> even better?

The thief who forgets there's no honor among <u>thieves</u>
will be left with no leaf when his love lifts his <u>leaves</u>.

But don't drop your guard:

The <u>chefs</u> told the <u>chiefs</u> to suspend their <u>beliefs</u>.

Or, to put that succinctly: When in doubt, look it up.

Then, too, there's this:

The plural form of a number, letter, or abbreviation gets apostrophe *s* ***('s)*** when it strives to become a plural:

<u>SINGULAR</u>	<u>PLURAL</u>
R	*The three R's*
6	*two 6's*
1980	*the 1980's*
IOU	*IOU's*

Additionally, English, like every other language, will occasionally throw a curve. And the ones that it throws simply have to be memorized. To pick two examples:

child/children; woman/women

Which leads us somewhat shakily into the realm of **collective nouns**, where the *word* is singular (it doesn't have any of the plural endings) but it means "more than one." Women and children aside (since they're *not* collective nouns) these include, among many others:

crowd, crew, equipment, information, collection, jury

When used in a sentence, you'll treat a collective noun as though it were singular. (Please see Agreement.)

There are other words, of course, that defy English grammar: *cactus/cacti; appendix/appendices; thesis/theses*, but a general rule applies:

WHEN IN DOUBT, LOOK IT UP.

<u>PREPOSITIONS</u>

A preposition is hard to define, but in general it's a word (or a very short phrase) that specifies the relationship between the nouns in your sentence and the rest of the action. Among the relationships described by prepositions are relationships of **time** (*before, after, during, until*); **space** (*above, below, on, in*); **direction** (*through, by, from, beyond, to*); **similarity** (*like*) and a whole variety of **companionable or adversarial relations** (*with, of, for, against, because of, in spite of, instead of, except*). The list goes on, but you get the idea.

These are a couple of prepositions at play:

The trainer went towards the enraged brontosaurus with a very big stick.
I approached my 30's with trepidation.
I promised I'd marry him before I learned he was a serial killer.
He found himself between the crocodile's teeth.
The wolf was at the door and leering at the tea cart.
This, then, is what we are fighting about.

Notice I ended that sentence with —oh (gasp) no!— a preposition. In up-tighter days, there used to be a rule: Never end a sentence with a preposition. The trouble with that rule was that no one could follow it and still sound human. Even Winston Churchill, no slouch when it came to language, rather famously thumbed his nose at it. "That," he declared firmly, "is one of the rules of English up with which I will not put."

Or to put that another way: The rule is something you don't have to put up with.

Why am I bothering you with stuff about prepositions? Because there's one rule you absolutely must (must!) obey:

WHENEVER YOU USE A PRONOUN AFTER A PREPOSITION,
IT MUST—REPEAT *MUST*—ALWAYS, INVARIABLY—
BE CHOSEN FROM THE LIST OF *OBJECTIVE* PRONOUNS.

(Please see Pronouns.)

PRONOUNS

A pronoun is a piece of shorthand, a symbol. It stands for, refers to, or takes the place of, a noun. The catch is a pronoun can only work clearly when your reader knows *which* noun you want it to stand for. Ask yourself always: Is it clear in this context? Are there too many other nouns strewn in its path? Does the pronoun correctly mirror the noun? (If the noun is "the reader" and your pronoun is "they," then your mirror is cloudy.) (Please see Agreement.)

According to the textbooks, there are many kinds of pronouns but we don't need to bother our pretty heads with them all now. Let's start with:

The 3 Basic Kinds Of Pronouns

Subjective Pronouns
Objective Pronouns
Possessive Pronouns

1. Subjective Pronouns (Column A)

These should be used when the pronoun is meant to be the subject of the sentence. The subject is either the person or the thing that's performing the action or enduring the state that your sentence is describing.

The pronoun is the subject in the following sentences:

I am leaving. You are stoned. She ate the tablecloth. They called the cops.

2. Objective Pronouns (Column B)

These should be used when the pronoun is meant to be the object of the action that's described in the sentence, or— please note— the object of a preposition. Just for example:

Jack called me. Mary dumped him and threw a meat axe at us.

	Column A Subjective Pronouns	Column B Objective Pronouns
Singular	I	me
	you	you
	he/she/it	him/her/it
Plural	we	us
	you	you
	they	them
Indefinite	who	whom

So far, no sweat. But where many people get into major trouble is when Jack decides to telephone two or more people and Mary tries to carve up everyone she knows. Then we get the following

Incorrect Constructions:

Jack called Estelle and I.

Mary tried to meat-axe he and Sebastian.

No no no no no no no. Or to put that another way: ***NO!***

He (the subject—chosen from Column A) can only call an object (chosen from Column B):

CORRECT CONSTRUCTIONS:

Jack called me.

Jack called Estelle and me.

Jack called Estelle, Cleopatra, Victoria, Alexandra and me.

Doesn't matter if all of Vassar comes between Jack and me, Jack still called *me*. (And *Mary killed him*.)

THERE ARE TWO BIG RULES ABOUT CHOOSING A PRONOUN.

RULE #1
NO MATTER HOW MANY PEOPLE OR WORDS GET IN ITS WAY, THE PRONOUN STAYS THE SAME.

If there's one rule you memorize, memorize that one, though you don't even have to. All you have to do, as I said once before, is to test-drive your sentences and listen to what you've said. And that's glaringly true with pronouns.

In the case of Jack's phone call (or any other act involving two or more people), say the sentence out loud, applying one simple trick:

Cut all the words between the verb and the pronoun (and similarly cut the words that come after the pronoun).

The verb here is "called," so in this case you're cutting out the words "Estelle and" and you'll find that what you've said in your first illiterate sentence was:

Jack called I.

And you've similarly informed the Admissions Office at Harvard that:

Mary axed he.

And since even to your own very fond and prejudiced ear, both sound ridiculous, jump to Column B.

All of which leads us to:

RULE #2
PRONOUNS AREN'T DISHES ON A CHINESE MENU. IN OTHER WORDS, YOU CAN'T PICK ONE FROM COLUMN A AND ONE FROM COLUMN B.

Meaning: if *any* word in Column A is right, it follows then that *every* word in Column A is right and, implicitly, every word in Column B is wrong. And the other way around. If a B word is right, all the B words are right and all the A words are wrong.

Therefore, you can't say "between her and I" (one from Column B and one from Column A) and similarly you ought to say "You gave the book to whom?" since you'd naturally make the statement "You gave the book to him" (and *him* and *whom* are both Column B).

If you're confused about exactly which pronoun to use in a particular sentence (and neither sounds right and neither sounds wrong) try reading down the list— substituting every other pronoun in the column for the one you want to use. If *any* of them sound wrong, then *all* of them are wrong, and you can jump to the other column.

Still confused after that? Okay:

Try the tip about cutting the extra words.

If you're tempted to perpetrate "between Rick and I," say aloud: "between I." Conversely, if you've uttered "Me and Joe went to school," try "Me went to school." Or else try reversing the whole order of your sentence. Would you say "There's a gulf between I and my friend?" If you wouldn't, then don't say "between she and I." (And if you would, you're in much deeper trouble than you know.)

Joe and I went to school.

There's suddenly a gulf between her and me.

3. POSSESSIVE PRONOUNS (COLUMN C)

Possessive pronouns are friendly fellows and rarely cause trouble. Possessive pronouns stand for possessive nouns and indicate ownership, i.e., possession, among other things.

COLUMN C

POSSESSIVE PRONOUNS

Preceding the noun:	Following (or instead of) it:
my	mine
your	yours
his/her	his/hers
its	its
our	ours
their	theirs
your	yours
whose	whose

NOTE: THERE ARE NO APOSTROPHES IN POSSESSIVE PRONOUNS.

("It's" means "it is," and "who's" means "who is." Please see Contractions.)

Examples of possessive pronouns at play:

Your outrageous clumsiness killed my desire.

The fault was yours; the cold comfort was mine.

Why are you standing on her esophagus?

Yes, I'm certain it was definitely hers.

The kitten, bedazzled by the moon, chased its tail while the hamsters, oblivious to danger, chased theirs.

This is his leaf, but the ant hill is ours!

Whose grackle is this?

So this is the boy whose heartstrings you plucked in 1967 in Ogunquit, Maine.

3 OTHER KINDS OF PRONOUNS

INDEFINITE

RELATIVE

REFLEXIVE

INDEFINITE PRONOUNS refer to one or more *unspecified* people (or, for that matter, things). There are three different groups of them, and each has its rules.

Group #1 includes, for example: *Everybody, nobody, anybody, anything, everything, something, anyone, everyone, someone, no one, either [one], each [one], every [one], much.*

All of these pronouns act as though they're singular when used in a sentence, even when their meaning implies "more than one." In other words, they always take the singular possessive and the singular (specifically, 3rd person) verb. (Please see Agreement.)

Either of his mistresses is capable of murder.

Each of your answers is equally absurd.

There are three different groups of them, and each has its rules.

Will everyone who left his fish on the trampoline please come and claim it?

Second thing to know: When any of these pronouns begin to become possessive, they do take apostrophes:

Is this your mackerel or somebody else's?

It's anybody's guess.

Group #2 (which encompasses *both*, *few*, *several* and *many*) will, on the other hand, always take the plural:

Several are missing. Few are replaceable.

Both of the Humperdinks completely lost their minds.

And here's another curve:

Group #3— *all, any, some, half, none, most* and *more*— can, in most guises, adapt to appease the noun, going singular or plural, depending on what's at stake.

Most/half/some/none/all [of the meal] was good.

Most/half/some/none/all [of the meals] were good.

None of the cake has been eaten by the boys.

None of the boys have been eaten by the wolves.

When any of these pronouns begin to become possessive...

When any of this lesson begins to put you to sleep...

Neither, like *none*, can occasionally be a coin toss. Purists (like me) will enjoin you to use the singular, but no one will shoot you if you happen to use the plural.

When the pronoun stands alone as the subject of the sentence, the singular is a must:

None of us is perfect. Neither has the edge.

But when the pronoun is qualified, you may (at your peril) go singular or plural, though you're certain to offend at least somebody either way:

Neither of the congressmen are or is running for reelection.

None of the panelists have or has anything to say.

And analyze the difference between these correct wordings:

Neither of the girls have rehearsed with their partners.

Neither of the girls has rehearsed with her partner.

Here's another insidious curve. When the pronoun "one" is the subject of the sentence, it always takes the singular.

One is rather hard put to name Caligula's virtues.

But when "one" is merely a number—as in "one of those nights"—then the actual subject of the sentence is the nights, which are obviously plural and agree with a (3rd person) plural verb.

He's one of those guys who take your number and never call. (Not *takes* and not *calls*.)

The way you can test it is to bury the "one of" and try the sentence without it.

Those guys who take your number and then never call [of whom he is one] would be a waste of your time anyway.

Agreed. This is one of those nasty tricks of grammar that make you hate grammar; let's leave it and move on.

RELATIVE PRONOUNS are links in the chain, relating the pronouns or nouns that precede them to the rest of the sentence. Examples are *that*, *which*, *who*, *whose* and *what* (when *what* is used in the sense of *that which* or *things that*).

As a safe general rule,
use *who* and *whose* when you're referring to people,
and *that*, *which* and *what* when you're referring to things.

What you choose to do with animals can vary with how you feel: Do you think they're closer to people? or merely closer to things?

Paris is the city that most amuses me.

The ascot that she'd turbulently tossed on the credenza lay crumpled in defeat.

The people who prefer anorexia to chocolate are a very peculiar lot.

The cobra, which was coiled on the boulder above the avalanche, was dreaming of fictive frogs.

The cat, who had a wonderful disposition and one eye, licked delightedly at her paw.

The crowd, whose disappointment was all too apparent, waved pennants and smashed cars.

Matilda always knew she could have what she wanted if only she were willing to get up off the couch.

We learn that what appear to be optical illusions are actually oases.

You'll note *that* and *which* can be generally interchangeable, but still, in some contexts, there's a difference between the two:

The knife that was sitting atop the mantelpiece was clean; the ones that she'd buried under the flowerbeds were not.

The *thats* in that sentence are specifically identifying, and not just describing, which knife it is you're discussing (the one displayed in the living room/ the ones interred in the garden). And in that case, the word that fits your purpose would be a *that.*

Now compare and contrast to this:

The knife, which was sitting atop the mantelpiece, was clean.

In this case, the *which* clause (and note: the thing is a clause and gets enclosed in a set of commas) is an incidental descriptive which doesn't affect the basic identity of the weapon.

REFLEXIVE PRONOUNS all end in "-self" or its plural form, "selves." As in *myself, yourself, himself, herself, itself, yourselves, ourselves, themselves.*

They're used to refer to the other nouns or pronouns that were previously used in the same sentence. They can't stand alone. Or to put that another way, never never ever use reflexive pronouns if you haven't mentioned one of their counterparts first.

Here's a thoroughly unforgivable **misuse** of the reflexive:

The president invited my wife and myself to attend the Inaugural.

No he didn't! Not even if you donated twenty billion dollars and your wife is his second cousin; that sentence never happened. What did happen was:

The president invited my wife and <u>me</u>...

Why? Read the rule. There was nothing in your first unfortunate formulation for the pronoun "myself" to reflect back *to*. In fact, the first mention of anything remotely related to your person came only at the point where you got the invitation... and thereupon became an objective pronoun. And again, you can test that by scaling back the sentence and yammering how "The president invited myself." And if *that* doesn't rankle you, I guess nothing will.

Here are some proper uses for reflexives:

The roaches were utterly beside themselves with pleasure when they came upon the breadcrumbs you'd scattered on the floor.

I hurt myself badly when I fell down the hole.

When the teacher told Miranda to "just be yourself," she wasn't yet aware that Miranda was a vampire.

The cannibal, feeling like a snack, ate himself.

Reflexive pronouns can also be used to add proprietary emphasis:

Face it, Othello, you yourself are to blame.

Even we ourselves didn't see it at the time.

Finally, there's a new kind of pronoun to contemplate:

THE POLITICALLY CORRECT PRONOUN.

Once upon a time in much simpler, though some would say sexist, times, the pronoun *he* stood for both men and women, i.e., humankind (and animal-kind too). And so we had the simple:

Every dog has his day.

Current fashion, however, would divert us into a quagmire of "sensitive" verbosity from which every sentence will emerge in legalese. To wit:

Every dog has his or her day.

Even worse, *Every chairman should be sure he has a chair* would succumb to *Every chair should be sure that he or she has a chair or a chairlette, as the case may be.*

However, take heart. There are two ways around it. The first is to simply thumb your nose at PC and choose grammatical, instead of political, correctness. The chicken-choice is simply to pluralize your nouns. So the questionable *Every student must buy his own books* can very simply become *Students must buy their own books*. And similarly:

Chairs should make sure they have chairs.

Though it still leaves us stuck with:

All dogs have their days.

(Please see Agreement.)

One final note:

PRONOUNS IN COMPARATIVES

When you're talking about someone who is A) taller than or B) quite apparently younger than you are— quick, choose your pronoun.

She's younger than ___. He's taller than ___.

The answer, in case you were wondering, is *I*. And the reason why it is, can be found in my initial sentence above. The implicit (though unstated) ending of your sentence is *than I (am.)* And the same rule holds when he, she or it is *as tall as I (am.)* Or is uglier than *he*, although handsomer than *they*. Or *knows more than we* (implicitly: *do*.)

Again, when in doubt, try saying your sentence and append the implicit verb. *He's taller than me am* just doesn't fly, and *He knows more than me do* proves that he does.

But caution:

Angelina is different from me. ("From" is a preposition and, well...see the Rule.)

AGREEMENT
(OR: CAN'T WE ALL JUST GET ALONG?)

In a complicated world, nouns and verbs, and nouns and pronouns, had to painfully figure out how to work together smoothly. And their ultimate decision was to heed basic rules.

Fortunately, for writers, they didn't invent many.

RULE #1

A VERB MUST INVARIABLY AGREE WITH ITS SUBJECT IN NUMBER AND PERSON AND, SIMILARLY, A PRONOUN MUST AGREE WITH ITS NOUN.

We've already defined "number." Unless we're dealing with Indefinite Pronouns (please see Pronouns), a noun or a pronoun is either singular (one) or plural (more than one). Those are the "numbers."

"Person" refers to a grammatical classification that actually applies to both nouns and verbs but begins with the nouns, or more illustratively, the pronouns. There are three such "persons."

The first person is *I*, the second person is *you*, the third person is either *he*, *she* or *it* (or their actual given names— Lemuel, Alexandra, San Pedro, guacamole). And again, speaking strictly in grammatical terms, the first person is the speaker, the second person is the spoken *to*, and the grammatical third person is the spoken *about*.

As, for example, when I turn to you and snipe, *"But of course you and I know that he is a louse."*

I am the speaker, *you* are the spoken to, and *he* is the louse.

With that under our belts, let's now define "person" along with "number."

	SINGULAR	PLURAL
Speaker:	1st Person: I	1st Person: we
Spoken to:	2nd Person: you	2nd Person: you
Spoken about:	3rd: he/she/it	3rd: they

We've just defined number and person for the *subject* (the noun or the pronoun) but what about the verb? Ah yes, verbs too have a number and a person. Let's start with a simple regular verb and then run it down the chart in the present tense.

	PRONOUN/NOUN	VERB
1st person:	Singular: I	Singular: slink
2nd person:	Singular: you	Singular: slink
3rd person:	Singular: he (etc)	Singular: slink**s**

	PRONOUN/NOUN	VERB
1st person:	Plural: we	Plural: slink
2nd person:	Plural: you	Plural: slink
3rd person:	Plural: they	Plural: skink

Your eye will immediately discern that in English every regular verb adds an *s* to—and only to— the 3rd person singular. Therefore, you can never observe that *She slink*, any more than you can wantonly boast that *I slinks*. (*I* is a 1st person singular pronoun but *slinks* is a 3rd person singular verb; they agree in "number" but not in "person." And Rule #1 is: they gotta do both.)

If you're batting a thousand so far in this game, remember that after pride cometh the fall. Most people, it would seem, bump smack into trouble when they try to arrange a pact between indefinite pronouns or collective nouns and the verbs they want to marry. As we've previously discussed, the verb form that works with almost all of these fellows is the 3rd person singular:

Each of the witches flies (not fly) on a broom.
Neither of us really has (not have) anything to lose.
The number of accidents was (not were) utterly appalling.

And meanwhile, don't forget to coordinate your pronouns:
Every man and boy is eventually called upon to prove his mettle.

Please recall the second part of the First Rule:

A PRONOUN MUST ALWAYS AGREE WITH ITS NOUN IN NUMBER AND PERSON.

SINGULAR NOUNS	AGREEABLE PRONOUNS
The reader	he (him, his)
The average American	he (him, his)
The audience	it (it, its)
PLURAL NOUNS	AGREEABLE PRONOUNS
Readers	they (them, their, theirs)
Americans	they (them, their, theirs)
Audiences	they (them, their, theirs)

The average *American* [implicitly, *he*] *is astounded when* *he* *sees* *his* *chiropodist weep.* [Not, *when they see their..*]

Americans [they] *drive* *their* *cars too fast.*

The *reader* [she] *will weep when* *she* *gets* *to page ten.*

Readers [they] *weep when* *they* *read about grammar.*

The *audience* [it] *fell asleep in* *its* *chairs.*

ANOTHER FORM OF AGREEMENT: THE QUESTION OF CLAUSES

A clause is a part of a sentence that may or may not make sense on its own. Whenever it depends on another clause in the sentence in order to make sense, the two clauses have to agree— about, among other things, who's doing what— or in other words, the verb has to marry the right noun. Examples may clarify:

After winning the foot race, his grandmother gave him a hug.

You've just sent his grandmother racing around the lawn and then hugging an idle boy. Not to say that's impossible, but according to your sentence it was grandma who did the winning. The rule being this:

THE FIRST NOUN OR PRONOUN THAT'S MENTIONED AFTER THE CLAUSE IS THE SUBJECT OF THAT CLAUSE.

So what you meant to say was this:

After he won the footrace, his grandmother gave him a hug.

Here's another atrocious thought:

After letting her hair down, the party was more exciting.

So I'm left with a hairy party who's parted its hair differently and thus had a better time. Or else:

After letting her hair down, she had more fun at the feast.

Here's another list of atrocities— and these you can fix yourself:

Being totally loaded, I wasn't able to move the car.

A man of exceptional genius, they asked him to fix the sink.

Adolescent and full of beans, the whole planet appeared to be his.

Walking and chewing gum, a sense of mastery filled her soul.

More About Possessives

Mere pages ago, it seems, we had a warm cozy chat about possessive pronouns, but obviously, a gerund can also get possessive, and so can a greedy noun.

The possessive form of a noun— which is usually accomplished by adding apostrophe *s* (*'s*)—is the general shape of a noun when it possesses, or otherwise deserves, does, measures (time, space or worth) or is the source of— or the focus of— another following noun, or another implicit noun. Thus:

<u>*Kevin's*</u> *tatoo was one of the artifacts of* <u>*Angela's*</u> *influence.*

And similarly, we're possessed by:

Dorian's portrait, tomorrow's meeting, the jury's verdict, a moment's notice, a dime's worth of difference, a good day's work, the narrative's tension, the student's suspension, the box's dimension, the writer's intention, the policy's critics, and the elephant's escape.

It was Mary's is —surprise!— a complete and credible sentence when it follows as an answer to: Whose axe is this? (A case in which the thing that's possessed is implicit.)

Okay. I know. This is boringly straightforward. Where woe wanders in is when the possessor ends in an *s*. And don't get me wrong here. The rule hasn't changed.

A singular possessive takes a simple apostrophe *s* no matter what your mother told you.

It does not— repeat not— take a silly dangling apostrophe and think that its work is done. So it's <u>not</u> *The boss' whim* (do you say it *the boss whim?* or do you say it *the boss-es whim?*) So...write it the way you say it:

My boss's stupid idea.

Imelda Marcos's shoes.

I spent the summer at Carlos's house.

There are very, very, very few exceptions to that rule and, as always, your tongue will guide you.

The heel of Achilles is pronounced as *Achilles' heel.* And the saying *for goodness' sake* can even be written *for goodness sake*, and you'll rarely get thrown in jail. As for Tennessee Williams' dramas, you can always play it by ear.

Yet another doorway to woe is often sprung when we deal with plurals, as in plural possessors. The rule is a piece of cake:

The proprietary apostrophe is added after the *s* that got added to form the plural.

Examples should make it clear:

Six Martians have landed. The spaceship belongs to all six Martians. Therefore, you'd talk about the *Martians' spaceship*. Your brothers share a bedroom. Therefore you'd talk about *my brothers' room*. But if each of your brothers has a bedroom to call his own, you'd refer to *my brothers' rooms*. Then, too:

The cities' budgets were eternally out of control and the taxpayers' money was frittered away on pork.

The Transylvanians' code of ethics involved never kissing a friend and, of course, never drinking on an empty stomach.

The singular exception to the rule of possessive plurals is the plural without an *s*.

The children's vaccination, the women's liberation, the gentlemen's agreement.

Here's another giddy exception: When the object of your concern belongs to several people jointly, the possessive apostrophe s arrives after— but *only* after—the second, or final, name:

Gilbert and Sullivan's opera was performed without respite in Simon and Ethel's den.

(William Gilbert and Arthur Sullivan communally wrote the opera, and Simon and Ethel communally own the den.)

But if Simon and Ethel split (after a shockingly messy spat about the lyrics to *Tit-Willow*) then the opera will be performed in both *Simon's and Ethel's dens*— on (at least one presumes) two separate occasions.

Similarly, too, *Lurch and Vampira's children* are the progeny of the couple, Lurch and Vampira. Though *Vampira's and Lurch's children* are distinctly repellent nouns that inhabit the same sentence, unrelated in terms of blood.

And one final example:

Her wing chair was covered with her cats' and dogs' fur.

(She has several cats and dogs and they each have a separate pelt.)

If she only had one of each, and they also had one of each, it's *her cat's and dog's fur.* Though of course, if they shared a pelt— say, a Siamese cat and dog?— one would have to observe the chair retained *her cat and dog's fur.*

Then, too, even a gerund can begin to get possessive if you haven't trained it to fawn:

Dancing's main virtue lies in stimulating the toes.

MISCELLANEOUS COMMON ERRORS

Shoulda, coulda, woulda...

Nothing is so dismaying as the commonly written *should of*— as *I should of seen it coming,* or *He would of opened the door.*

If you've committed these sins to paper, you've been writing a kind of phonetics that simply doesn't work on the page. Yes, that's the way it sounds, but it isn't the way it looks, and it isn't the way it functions.

Should is a modal verb whose rough synonym might be *ought.* *Of* is a preposition that expresses a form of relationship that connects a couple of nouns. And just for example: *ace of spades, son of a gun, side of a barn, a couple of nouns.* It's therefore nearly impossible to come up with a logical sentence that incorporates *should of,* but nonetheless, I'll give it a try:

This is the should of shoulds: You should follow the Golden Rule.

Or:

The fastest horse in the race was the 3-year-old filly Should of the Pegasus Stables.

What you're going for, of course, is the modest *should have,* whose contracted form would be *should've,* which sounds mightily like *should of,* except that it isn't.

The proper usage of "use"...

Similarly, a phrase like *I use to play the piano* is what you hear but not what you write. *Use* means to utilize. Therefore, while you might employ mittens or strong drink in your efforts to tackle Gershwin, (*This is what I use to play the piano*) that isn't quite what you mean. *I used to play the piano* connotes that you formerly did. *I used to be a soprano* connotes that you formerly were. But hark! In some negatives— the ones that involve a *did*— the proper phrasing becomes *use. I didn't use to be such a drag*. Although, on the other hand: *I never used to be catty*. (No *did*, so no *use*.)

Which leads us into:

Contractions.

Improperly used apostrophes can sprout like stalactites in the frozen waste of your prose. Contractions get grammatically interchanged with possessives or even with common verbs and the result is an awful mess. So let's begin with contractions (as it happens I just did, since *let's* is the everyday contraction of *let us*). When used in contractions, the apostrophe tells the reader that a letter, or several letters, were removed at the very spot where that apostrophe left its mark. For example:

Long Way	Contraction	Missing Links
let us	let's	u
I have	I've	ha
we are	we're	a
we had	we'd	ha
would not	wouldn't	o
they are	they're	a
they would	they'd	woul
there would	there'd	woul
there had	there'd	ha
who is	who's	i
who has	who's	ha

Notice apostrophe-*d* ('d) can interchangeably indicate a *had* or a *would*—just as ('s) can be an *is* or a *has*— with only context to make it clear.

There'd have been no America if there'd been no Columbus.

That's all that's been said.

The following are some major sources of confusion:

CONTRACTION	PRONOUN
it's	its
who's	whose
they're	their

The monster told us that it's absolutely wrong to write about its mere pecadillos or its fangs.

Who's the person who's misused the unpardonable pronoun whose provenance we decried?

They're sure of their winning it, but little do they know.

Let's be sure that the supervisor lets us have our lunch.

In the matter of Who v. Whom...

There are many grammatical rules about the usage of who and whom, only nobody ever remembers what they are. Which gives you a little leeway to utterly misuse them since no one'll know you did.

Technically *whom* is the objective form of *who* and (please see the chart) should be used in whatever spot you'd use *him, her* or *them*. But the rule is so barnacled with bloody exceptions that it's easier to remember the seventeenth stanza of *The Star Spangled Banner* than to trot them all out. So just try to remember this:

When in doubt, use *who*. It's the generally acceptable default position in almost any sentence *except* when it comes at the tail of a preposition:

To Whom It May Concern

For whom the bell tolls.

With whom did he arrive?

And

Who did what to whom?

From bad to worse...

Bad is an adjective (it applies to, and only to, the nouns in your sentence). *Badly* is an adverb (it applies to, and only to, the verbs in your sentence). You may not interchange them.

Alexandra felt bad means the lady was either sorry or generally out of sorts, while the phrase *She felt badly* means that after she burned her fingers on the hot butterscotch sauce, her sense of touch was slightly impaired.

Bad refers to *her* (the noun in your sentence); while *badly* refers to *felt* (the verb in your sentence).

Ask yourself, therefore, before you append a *ly* to any statutory adjective (thus, automatically, turning it into an adverb) if it really applies to the verb.

The android looked obsequious.

The android looked obsequiously at the board of the master computer.

6.

GIVING CREDIT WHERE IT'S DUE (AND A FOOTNOTE ABOUT FOOTNOTES)

Ideas are property. They're owned by whoever originally thought them. Prose is property. Phrases that are apt enough or clever enough to quote are the signed-and-sealed property of whoever it was who wrote them. Plagiarism is theft. And the imperative commandment is:

THOU SHALT NOT STEAL.

Thou mayest, however, borrow. The question arises as to how to give credit when you're using somebody else's word-for-word prose or the nugget of his ideas, and, depending on the context, there are several ways to do it.

Let's imagine you've written this:

A review of the material will suddenly yield the insight that Stalin's propaganda was based on Pavlov, and Hitler's, on Freud.

Well, aren't you the clever one! I mean, what a neat, incisive observation— except that it isn't yours and you've covertly implied it was. And while it's hypothetically possible, at least on occasion, that "great minds think alike," it's astronomically unlikely that they'll think *exactly* alike or that the general run of sophomores is up to that kind of speed. And morality aside (and it should never be pushed aside) you're almost certain to get caught.

You've heard the thought somewhere, but imagine (Scenario One) that you can't remember where. And a maddening bout of research doesn't turn up a single clue. At least in some contexts, you can always revert to this:

According to one analyst, Stalin's propaganda was based on Pavlov, while Hitler's was based on Freud.

Now suppose (Scenario Two) you eventually track it down:

It was Jacques Ellul's theory that Stalinist propaganda...

Which produces another question: will the major part of your audience know who Jacques Ellul is? And if not, can you help them out?

The French social psychologist Jacques Ellul, observed...

Or does the context (say, an academic paper) require more?

In his book "Propaganda," the French social psychologist Jacques Ellul observed that...

Note: because you're merely paraphrasing Ellul, quotation marks would be out (because you aren't using his words).

On the other hand, if you are, then you'd have to proclaim it thus:

But as the French social psychologist Jacques Ellul observed, "Stalinist propaganda was in great measure founded on Pavlov's theory of the conditioned reflex. Hitlerian propaganda was in great measure founded on Freud's theory of repression and libido."

Is the passage, as he said it, too long for your present needs? You can legally make it shorter, but only if you indicate *where* you've omitted words (by the use of elipses—three little dots) and by bracketing words you've added to preserve the flow of the thought:

"Stalinist propaganda was in great measure founded on Pavlov's theory... [Hitler's] in great measure was founded on Freud's..."

If you're writing, for example, a magazine article, either version should be enough. But for an academic paper, you're required to cite the source. This is done by adding a footnote— a note at the foot of the page that gives the author, title and date. If the source is a printed book, add the publisher and the page. If the source is a magazine, add the name of the publication and the month as well as the year. If the publication's a Journal, add the Volume, Issue, and page.

You'll indicate there's a footnote by appending a tiny number at the end of the cited text. I.e.:

...founded on Freud's ..." [1]

And no, this excrescence of amazingly dull minutiae isn't quite over yet, but (sorry) you need to know it. Along with a little Latin:

IBID AND OP CIT

Ibid —or its briefer abbreviations *ib.* and *id.*— is Latin for "the

---

1 Ellul, "Propaganda: The Formation of Men's Attitudes," Knopf, 1968, p 5

same source I gave in the last footnote" or, in other words, "ditto." If, for example, immediately after quoting a passage from *Propaganda*, on the same page or another, you quote from the same book, you'd give it another footnote, but simply type *ibid* instead of repeating the text.

Op cit, also Latin, means "opus cited," or "I already told you where I got it from, folks, and I ain't gonna tell you again." In a footnote, *op cit* follows the author's name. Nor does it matter if you first mentioned the opus 70 pages before. The second time you quote it, you give it another footnote, type in the fellow's name, and then dismiss it with *op cit* (as long as you're still quoting from the book you mentioned before).

Sic Transit Sic

Here's how it goes: When you believe there's an error (of fact, or even spelling) in whatever it is you're quoting, use *sic*, in brackets, at the point where the error occurs. "Sic" means "thus," as in "Thus it appeared in the writer's original writing so nobody blame *me*." Just for example:

According to her resumé, she's "a graduate, with honors, from Yail [sic] University," where she majored in English.

Last gasp on citations.

Suppose you have to quote an even longer verbatim passage than the ones quoted above. In that case, the custom is to set it off on its own— by—take your pick: widening the margins, single-spacing the text (in the course of a standard manuscript), using a different font (or a smaller point of the same one), or doing it all in italics. The lead-in to the quote customarily ends in a colon, and quotation marks are redundant; the layout announces "quote." And so, just for example—

Dr. Elizabeth Whelan, president of the American Council on Science and Health, said this in a recent article:

> *If, as we suspect, Mayor Bloomberg is referring to deaths caused by exposure to secondhand smoke in restaurants and bars, the estimate of 1,000 deaths prevented [by smoking bans] is patently absurd... There is no evidence that any New Yorker —patron or employee—has ever died as a result of exposure to smoke in a bar or restaurant... The link between secondhand smoke and premature death...is a real stretch.*[2]

Note, too, that if the article you're quoting is on the net, it's academic courtesy to provide its complete address so as not to send your fact-checkers prowling for hard copy.

Finally, with the exception of public domain documents, there's a tight legal limit on how, when, why and how many words you can quote in a published book or article without infringing on copyright. Even if you properly attribute the quote to its source.

Depending on the context, the generally (but not always legally) accepted standard is 250 words.

The copyright page of the book— the one that you never look at (it's usually on the left-hand second or fourth page) will very likely spell out the rules.

ALL RIGHTS RESERVED.
No part of this book may be reproduced
or transmitted in any form or by any means,
electronic or mechanical, including, but
not limited to, photocopying, recording,
scanning, and e-mailing, nor stored
in any information and retrieval system
without prior permission in writing
from the publisher, except in the case of
brief quotations used in critical articles or reviews.
For permission, please address:

This limit to "free" words applies to anything written, not only to published books, but to magazine, newspaper or web log articles, and even to written material that hasn't been published yet (copyright attaches to the provable fact of authorship). Don't mess around. For more information on the limits of "fair use," check the copyright office:

http://www.copyright.gov/fls/fl102.html

There are, however, no free words when it comes to lyrics. I once paid fifty bucks to quote a total of twelve words; and Mick Jagger wanted ten times as much for a half a dozen.

(I decided to skip the quote.)

---

2 "Smoked out: Mayor Bloomberg Exaggerates Secondhand Smoke Risk," Whelan, Facts & Fears, American Council on Science and Health, Dec. 12, 2002, www.acsh.org/facts-fears/newsID.215/news_detail.asp

PART II:
SURVIVAL WRITING
CONTRACTS
BUSINESS LETTERS
EMAILS
STRATEGIC WRITING
RESUMÉS
PITCHES

7.
GETTING DOWN TO BUSINESS: STRATEGIC WRITING

Start with this premise: good business writing is basically indistinguishable from good nonbusiness writing. Like any form of writing it requires coherent logic, rigorous organization, and a knowing adherence to the same Four Commandments: be clear, be exact, be natural, be brief.

In fact, there's only one big difference between the two. Business writing has an ulterior motive (you want something, don't you?) so *good* business writing is therefore the kind of writing that gets you what you want.

If one of the things you want is to sell someone something (yourself, your services, your wares, your ideas) then getting what you want demands two separate skills. The first is good writing; the second is good strategy. And strategy itself demands two separate skills: Understanding the market (the market you're competing in) and, equally important, understanding your reader (the person you're writing *to*). Or to put that succinctly:

STRATEGY = MARKETING + PSYCHOLOGY.

Psychology is the ability to psych your reader out. To put yourself in his[1] shoes . To look at the situation from his (and not simply your own) point of view.

Please note I said "psych." I didn't say "sell." Because selling doesn't work. At least, selling that looks like selling doesn't work. And the give-aways of "selling that looks like selling" are meaningless adjectives, see-through promises, glowing generalizations and egotistical bloat—smoke

1 PC alert! Because finding a way around it is simply too dispiriting and syntactically alarming, I'm using the grammatically (but alas not politically) correct pronoun "he" to stand for both sexes. To those who are offended, I suggest a rereading of the section on pronouns back in Chapter 5, and perhaps a nice walk around the block to clear your head.

without heat; legs without feet.

The reason you can't do it is because it doesn't work, and the reason it doesn't work is that the person you're writing to is fairly sophisticated, at least in his field. (If not, he wouldn't be in a position in his field to do you any good, and you wouldn't be writing him.)

(Which isn't to say that the person you're writing to isn't, just as possibly, an unremitting jerk, it's simply to say that you can't *count* on it. Therefore, you have to approach your reader as though he's at least as intelligent as you. And if *you're* too advanced to think baloney is sirloin, then figure so's he.)

In other words, you have to offer substance as well as style and specifics in addition to realistic generalizations. And again, you have to do it with clarity and speed, since your reader (Important Executive that she is[2]) is a lot too busy to slog through a veritable swamp of excessive prose, or go back and read it again, trying vainly to catch your drift.

And remember something else: You're asking this person to take a gamble on a stranger. It's a gamble that, initially, will cost him money and time, and could, if he bets wrong, even cost him his own job. So you have to reassure him as well as convince him. And again, you have to look at it from his point of view. Which gets us, forthwith, to a basic rule of the road:

YOUR READER ISN'T AT ALL CONCERNED WITH WHAT YOU WANT, HE'S CONCERNED WITH WHAT *HE* WANTS.

Your prospective employer doesn't give a hot flyer that *you* need a job; his concern is exclusively that *he* needs a job done. Nor is he susceptible to helium-filled boasts that you're an absolute genius with a breakthrough idea and you only need a break; what concerns him is... whether it'll make him any money.

Nor is this altered when the business he's engaged in is loosely called The Arts. The hard fact is that while *you're* doing Art, *he's* doing Business, and the twain have to meet. Which doesn't mean you have to dumb down your art but rather that you do have to smarten up your pitch.

---

2 There! I got a "she" in.

Just for example:

You're a young photographer. You're the next Ansel Adams or Cartier-Bresson. You want this assignment because a) you need the money and b) the exposure and c) the opportunity to indulge your obsessive-compulsion for perfection— or to put that another way, you want to do Art.

Here's what the guy who's going to hire you wants. He wants to know you'll show up on time and be awake, that you'll actually cover all the shots he's assigned, that the work will be adequate and actually usable, that you'll do it on deadline, and not give him grief. If you *also* give him Art, he may, if you're lucky, not hold it against you.

Or that's how it goes about ninety percent of the time.

The point is, in order to get what you want (money, exposure, a chance to do your stuff) you first have to convince him— in his kind of language, from his point of view— that *he'll* get what *he* wants.

If it happens that he doesn't know what he wants, then you'll have to convince him— again in his terms— that he wants what you've got.

Or to spin that again, as the award-winning screenwriter Robert Towne put it, "When you can't do what they want, you have to convince them that they want what you did."

And the same rule applies no matter what it is you're after. Whether it's a job as an office manager, a paralegal, a salon colorist, or an editor-in-chief. Whether it's a grant to pursue your advanced studies on the mating habits of gerbils, or a contract to service the Coke machines at the zoo, or a catalogue entry for your hand-painted shoes.

(What's in it for the catalogue? What's in it for the zoo?)

All of which leads us to the marketing part of the pitch.

Marketing Is Not Just A Seat-of-the-pants Job; It's A Job That Requires Research.

Whoever it is you're writing to is not a "generic company" but a very specific shop, with its very specific needs. So you probably can't convince them with a gauzy "generic pitch." (Or at least the odds are against you.)

What *are* their specific needs?

What *are* their specific goals?

What problems have they been having?

And how would you, specifically, help them to reach their goals (or help them to solve their problems)?

Your research could take you to your local library (the Business Department) or an online ramble through their annual reports and the business columns of papers, or a chat with a savvy broker.

Obviously, the basic part of Marketing is...Marketing: understanding the market, by which I mean, theirs. Who are their customers? Who is their competition? And what has their competition been doing better than they? (How could they bridge the gap? and how could you help them do it?) Futhermore, how does your invention or service align with the current market? What's the popular demand for, say, hand-painted shoes? or why— on what solid marketing basis— are they on the way In?

A final thing to research is your own competition. What specific edge have you got? And what can you specifically do that the others can't?

The fact that you've immersed yourself in doing the basic research— that you've illustrated your interest and your dedication to Them— is an edge-and-a-half in itself.

Not every situation seems to call for elaborate research, but every situation demands that you do some.

Don't ever think you can wing it. That dog doesn't fly.

8.
THE BUSINESS OF LETTERS

Business letters are simply letters about business. The only thing that inclines you to think they're a separate species is the slight adjustment in tone ("businesslike" is the word) and the minor but messy detail that their subject is life or death.

If you've grown up believing email is the height of communication and the soul of The Way We Are, well. . . ROTFLMAO, it's time to discuss letters.

START WITH THE RIGHT PAPER.

Before you've written a word, the first statement you make—in other words, the body-language of your letter— is the paper it's written on and the envelope it comes in.

Begin with a good paper— 50 pound at least, 8½ x 11 inches, with a smooth clean surface compatible with your printer. White, tan or cream are the characteristic colors, though you might, on occasion, have a logical reason to stray. (Like, for instance, your name is Green, or your store is The Pink Lady.) Get envelopes that match.

The next question is letterhead. If your writing paper is personal, your letterhead should include your name, address, phone number and, optionally, email. If your letterhead's for your business, you might want to add a logo— a small graphic emblem of. . . whatever it is you do— and a web address if you've got one.

Designing a letterhead is either easy or hard, depending on your abilities, your bank account and your eye. If you're looking for inspiration, start by browsing in stylish stationers or visiting local print shops. All of them offer sample books with sample layouts and fonts and suggestions for company logos. You can buy their wares at a price, or you can replicate their ideas by playing around on your own computer, finding public domain clip-art, and shopping for fonts on line. The envelope, too, should have your printed name and address— in the upper left corner— in the same font as your letter's.

And now that we're on the subject—

The Envelope, Please.

It embodies the First Impression. It either says "Open me" or "(Yawn) put me aside." It can even announce the salient characteristics of its sender so you don't want it yelling "Slob!" Here's where your good quality paper pays for itself, where the tan of your envelope pops from a pile of white, and where the font in your address corner pleases somebody's eye. Do *not* address it with labels. Either type the reader's address or else write it with a clean-looking, unaffected hand and with a pen that isn't a ballpoint.

And always address your letters to an actual human name— meaning not to a "Managing Editor," "Children's Buyer" or "Personnel." If you aren't sure of the name, call the company switchboard and ask, and if the name appears "gender-neutral" (is a "Kerry" a he or she? [3]) or if its spelling defies phonetics (Mr. Kristal or Mr. Kristol or Mr. Cristal or Mr. Crystal?) now's the moment to get it straight.

The proper way of addressing the outside of an envelope proceeds, top to bottom, from the most to the least specific, so, just for a quick example, it's:

Mr. Bob Cratchit
Accounting Department
Marley & Scrooge Ltd.
The Templeton Annex
127 Albemarle Road
London, England SW7

The rare minor exception to the "must have a name" rule is when you're writing to institutions— like, for instance, the IRS or the accounting department at Sears.

---

3 If you can't, for some reason, catch a clue to your reader's sex, never never make an assumption. Instead of a Mr. or Ms, just address it to "Kerry Stuart" or "Sandy Wilson" or "Ashton Fork". If your recipient has a title (like Professor, Doctor or Chairman) then your problem is happily solved and your solution can carry over to the greeting line of your letter (as in, Dear President Wilson...Corporal Stuart ...Reverend Fork)..

THE BASIC SHAPE OF A LETTER

Presuming you've got a letterhead, this is the general form:

1. The date.
2. The recipient's name and address (as shown on the envelope).
3. The greeting. (The "Dear Mr. X.")
4. If appropriate, the subject of your letter. ("Re: Acct # 275.")
5. The text.
6. The closing. (The "Best regards" or "Sincerely.")
7. Your written signature.
8. Your typed name.
9. If appropriate, your list of enclosures. ("Enc: CARB Report")

All letters are single-spaced; skip a line between each item. The date line is usually, but not necessarily, somewhere off to the right. After that, there are standard formats: Everything flush left (in which case, you'll skip a single line between paragraphs) or paragraphs indented (5 spaces, please) and with or without skipping any lines between paragraphs.

Let's deal with our running-order items one at a time.

THE OPENING

ONE: There's a reason to properly date your letters. First, it's an easy reference. (You can subsequently babble about "my letter of April 3rd.") It also serves as a semi-official diary of back-and-forths, and may even be legally crucial. (*So Your Honor, as you can see, I sent the samples on April 12th.*)

TWO: The name-and-address is really more than a formal gesture. Your letter, minus its envelope, can travel from desk to desk, so it's important to make it obvious whose desk it arrived at first. Then, too, there are legal reasons. (*As you see here, Your Honor, it was sent to the right address.*)

THREE: The greeting. The standard remains "Dear" but after that, you can get into trouble.

When you don't know your reader's sex (see Envelope footnote 3) and when you can't find a handy title (like *Doctor, Chairman* or *Dean*), the best, and the only, answer is to go with the full name— as in *Dear Terry Hopplekopf* or *Dear I.M. Pei*. Poor Terry Hopplekopf is used to the ruse by now, but he (or she) may forgive it lightly.

The only thing to never, ever do in a first letter is to stop with the first name. A "Dear Terry" aimed at a person with whom you've never conversed before is an unforgiveable act of presumption. How dare you! will be his response. (Or hers, as the case may be.)

The "Dear [total name]," though it still strikes me as awkward, is occasionally less awkward than the other forms of address, straddling, as it does, the gap between the formality of "Dear Mme. Defarge" and the intimate (or presumptively intimate) "Dear Therese." It works when, for example, you're writing to someone you've met but whom you don't actually *know*, or when you're writing to utter strangers on the cue of a mutual friend.

Yet another problem awaits— once again leaving you frozen like a "dear" caught in the headlights— when you're writing to faceless mobs. How do you open a letter to a store or a public agency, or to what you know is a hive of yawning clerks in a corporate maw?

The old standby is *Dear Sirs*, or the more collegially-worded *Gentlemen*, but standard official greetings haven't quite kept up with the times wherein the chances are fairly good that the dearest "Sirs" are the lovely ladies (and perhaps the order of ladies who'll think you're sexist and burn your note). *To whom it may concern* remains another acceptable wheezer, but the post-modernist answer is the post-sexual twist: *Dear Customer Services*; *Dear IRS*. Finally, there's a move to simply scuttle the false endearments and propel to the point with "To:" (as in *To: Billing Department; To: Lost and Found*).

Plurals present problems. (Letters sent to more than one person and meant for all.) *Messrs.* (which is drolly pronounced "messers") is two Misters, though there isn't a plural for Ms. If your letter is meant for two masculine readers of equal stature with an equal stake in its contents and an equal need for the note, you can either extend your greetings to *Mr. Tweedle and Mr. Dee* or to the *Messrs. Tweedle and Dee*. If your letter is meant for three or more people of equal stature and again with an equal interest, you could simply greet them as *Gentlemen* or *Dear Ladies and Gentlemen*, or possibly *Dear Colleagues, Dear Members*, or *Dear friends*.

CC's— which rather quaintly stand for yesterday's "carbon copies"— should be used when your correspondence is meant for the addressee but you're including several others on the basis of FYI. In which case, the greeting line is only to Person One, though the roster of those you've copied should be plainly listed at top (right under the main address) or else buried under your signature.

FOUR: We're up to the *Re:* which is short for the Latin "regarding" (or more literally, "here's the thing") and might easily be replaced with a simple English "About:" The reason to use the Re: is for instant communication, most often of something technical but nevertheless important. For example, *Re: Purchase Order 7-72* tells the billing department instantly the crucial fact in the game and makes it easy to find it later without an archeological dig. *Re: Lost Luggage, Flight 70, March 3* is your entire tale in a nutshell, saving everyone lots of time.

Similarly, a *Re: Your letter of April 12th* tells your reader immediately what it is you're referring to and what, to make sense of it, he has to dig from his files. On the other hand, don't use a Re: for the wrong reasons or to hit your host on the head. The first line of your letter should convey the point of your note.

THE MESSAGE

FIVE: The text. More on this later, but these are the general rules:

Choose the right tone. There's a human being on both ends of a letter. You're talking to *a person*, and simultaneously conveying your own personality, or lack thereof. Don't be a stiff, but don't be chatty. If you're complaining about something, don't be a boor. Ask yourself always, "How would I myself react to this letter?" and consider how the tone of it contributes to what you'd feel:

Dear Mr. Wimp: I regret to inform you that your qualifications do not meet our standards.

My toes have been stepped on; my outcry is Ouch!

Dear Mr. Wimp: Thank you for applying to Quagmire & Drudge. I'm so sorry that we don't have an opening for you now but we really need a salesman who can speak Japanese.

My response there is, Oh. My toes are intact because the tone here is tactful, even arguably humane.

Even small subtle choices can effect a warmth or a chill. Even something as simple as the formal "do not" as opposed to the easy "don't " can put the chill into a sentence.

Dear Mr. X— I do not have the time to do an ad for your store now...

(He will never call you again.)

Dear Mr. X— I'm truly sorry that I don't have the time to do an ad for your store now...

Words have a temperature, even on the page. And the eye can detect it just as clearly as if the words had little numbers around their necks. 98.6 is the temperature of a normal, healthy human word. Above that, it's fevered; below that it's icy, mechanical or dead.

Keep the thing short. Unless it's a letter that requires a lot of details, keep it to one page, and make every word "tell." The longer your letter is, the longer it will sit around waiting in the in-box. You're writing for a reason. Get to it. Fast.

State the purpose of your letter in your opening sentence (and do it without resorting to the words "I'm writing"). Instead of, for instance, *I'm writing to inquire...* try *I'm looking for information about...* or *Can you tell me where...?*

Begin with the bottom line. Before you tell the woes of your experience with the plumber, get to the point first: *Your workmen's misjudgment turned a leak in my kitchen into a tsunami that ruined the hall floor. The estimated cost of repairing this damage is $1400, which I do expect you to pay.*

Then, too, if it's you who've goofed, before you launch into your collection of swell excuses and resort to your violin, state your bottom line at the top: *Regretfully, we'll need to have a three-day extension on the deadline of May 1st.*

Dispense with long paragraphs. Break them into two. Even if it means you have to do it arbitrarily. Dense type is depressing.

Include all the relevant (but only the relevant) details. Account numbers, purchase numbers, file numbers, dates. Make it easy for your reader to comply with your request.

Your final paragraph should specify an action (on your part or theirs) if an action is required. So either state specifically what you'd like done, or what you plan to do. If you need to have your letter answered by a deadline, specify your deadline. Instead of the general *Let me know soon*, try, *Please let me know by the 7th at the latest, since I'll need that lead time to order the supplies.* And you might add, optionally, *If I haven't heard from you, I'll call you on the 6th.*

If possible, try to leave the ball in your court. Instead of *I'd like to get together to discuss it* (wherein you're left eternally waiting for a call), if appropriate, *I'll call your office next week to see if we can set up a time to discuss it.*

THE END GAME

SIX: The closing. Which almost inexorably leads you to *Sincerely* which is better than *Yours truly* (what on earth would that *mean*?) while *Cordially* comes off as a little bit warmer but still not presumptive. *Best regards* often does it; *My best* is another turn, though the latter are more appropriate when the reader's someone you know. A good way around it — especially in a letter of either inquiry or request— is to simply say *Thanks* or, more formally, *Thank you.* And similarly a thank-you note could end with a *Gratefully*, or even *Appreciatively,* or just *Thanks again.*

Or how about this: No closing at all! End your letter, sign your name. Though it isn't appropriate in every situation, it's a fine solution in others. If you've just fired someone or threatened him with a lawsuit, "sincerely" and "regards" become downright perverse. Like saying "Drop dead. And have a nice day."

Neither **SEVEN** (your signature) nor **EIGHT** (typed name) should require an explanation.

NINE: The enclosures. Listing them has a reason. First, so your reader will be aware of what you've sent. Second, if something's missing (accidents do happen) he'll know what to ask for. And finally, once again, perhaps for a legal reason. (*As you see here, Your Honor, I sent him the signed contract on February 8th.*)

A final bit of caution:

Be Careful What You Write.

Paper has a half-life of several thousand years (the Dead Sea Scrolls are still around) and your words can come back to haunt you. They can talk behind your back— get shared where they're not supposed to be, and are (as many jailbirds and the newly-divorced attest) nearly impossible to deny. The moral remains this:

It's Better To Speak The Unspeakable Than To Write It.

So now let's deal with specifics— the actual kinds of letters that you actually have to chain yourself to the radiator to write. Listed below, though in no particular order of either dreadfulness or dread, are:

The Ten Most Horrible Letters To Have To Write

¶ The "I Need a Job" Letter

This onerous little task comes in three different flavors: The Warm Solicitation (you know there's an open job, or you've got a recommendation), the Cold Solicitation (you're shooting into the void) and The Answer to Somebody's Ad. In all of these cases, your opening paragraph is death in the afternoon— a make-or-break moment when everything's on the line, and your reader either will or will not read further. In fact, it's so important I've reserved an entire section to talk about opening lines. Be patient, it's coming soon.

Your next problem is tone: striking the right note between groveling and bragging, between under- and overstating, between cuteness and rigor mortis. You might try the trick of pretending you're in the office and just conversing across the desk. Write it the way you'd say it. Try to picture the other person. Who do you think she is? What are the characteristics you believe would go with her job? Play to those characteristics. Or think of the kind of person you'd be more than happy to work with, and write your letter to *her.*

The meat of your letter is, of course, your qualifications and how your qualifications converge with the company's needs. Here's where your research should help you target your pitch. Highlight the strongest, most relevant parts in your resumé; offer additional details, or add an additional flourish— something *not* on your resumé that might, nonetheless, be appropriate to the job. You might want to talk about your general philosophy, your approach to the business, or its upcoming trends:

Though Sprockets & Lint hasn't yet gone global, there's a rapidly growing market for lint in Madrid and I believe, from my experience in Spain, I can crack it.

But caution: You have to be terse and specific. Two to four paragraphs is all that it ought to take to assert your qualifications.

And never, in any case, deal in a negative.

Wrong: *While I don't have experience in fashion, I've worked in cosmetics.*

Right: *My experience with Revlon and Chou involved high fashion ad shoots for which I coordinated clothes and accessories and worked very closely with the top-end designers.*

Finally, if you can't offer anything more specific than the sum of your past experience, remember that they're always in the market for "hard workers," "willing learners" and "team players." (How willing you are to work, learn, and play is another matter, but for now, sit on your tongue.)

If you're answering an ad, you're one up and three down. "Up" lies in knowing what they need, what they're after, what they do and who they are. "Down" lies in knowing they'll be inundated with letters, and the competition is fierce.

First, use the Re: (*Re: Your Reporter ad, June 23rd*) and get instantly to the point. Show how your qualifications mesh delightfully with their dreams:

Dear Mr. X: I have twelve years of experience at (whatever it is you want), speak Tagalog fluently, and don't require sleep.

And, just by the way, if you don't have the qualifications, or easily seven-eighths of them, don't answer the ad. Out in the naked city, there are 70,000 Zombies, speaking unimpeachable Tagalog, with endless wells of experience in…(whatever it is he wants). So unless you can drop the name of his brother-in-law or his client, save your postage and save your pride.

Here's an actual recent ad:

Creative, aggressive, experienced art director to lead us into the next new wave of the new year. Strong background in [specific area of design]. Fax letter, resumé, and salary needs to: [a fax number; no company name or identification].

No research is possible. You haven't the faintest clue as to who paid for the ad, and to whether or not you're casting your jewels before swine or your pigtails before Tiffany.

Your work is cut out for you. *Experienced*, you can manage (as long as you've got experience), *creative*— a junk adjective that dwells in beholders' eyes— you can still hope to illustrate by citing specific work, and the *wave* can be ridden by expressing an edgy style, but what on earth do they mean by *aggressive*? How's an art director aggressive? ("I knee-capped the copywriter and mat-decked the client"?) Perhaps they're eager to know you're on the make to corral business. Perhaps they want to know you're a leader with bold ideas. Interpret it as you will or, more elastically, as you can, but you can't entirely duck it.

As for "salary requirements" (or "salary history"—another abysmal ploy) it's a bear trap and you know it. *Salary: Negotiable* is one angle around it; another offers a range: *$X,000-$Y,000, depending on the specifics.* As for "salary history," sure, go on, you can add a couple of grand but understand they expect you to add a couple of grand, and you're both into Liar's Poker.

The wind-up to any of these letters is quick and plain. *I'm enclosing a resumé.* At most you can add something neutrally non-pushy: *And, of course, I'll be happy to answer any questions.* But never add a presumption like *I hope to hear from you soon…I look forward to hearing from you/ working with you/ meeting you.* All of which are likely to elicit a *Fat chance!*

And yes, I know. Increasingly you're asked to email your letter along with (a pdf of) your resumé, but— no difference— the same rules apply. The subject line remains *Your ad for a salesman/ Your ad in The Times.* If anything, the email should induce greater economy (see the chapter on Email) but not greater sloppiness or breeziness of tone.

Meanwhile, now that we've talked about the middle and the end of your letter...let's get back to the beginning and your crucial opening gambit.

Scenario #1:

Somebody's recommended you or said "You can use my name."

When You're Given A Name To Drop, Drop It Instantly; First Words.

Dear Mr. X: Fyodor Dostoyevsky told me you needed an editor and thought that you'd like my work.

There is no way on earth that that letter will not get read. Even if it's opened by a second assistant clerk. Even if she doesn't know who Fyodor Whatsis is, she wouldn't dare to just spindle it on the chance that Mr. Whatsis is the publisher's dearest friend. Nor will the guy you're sending it to give it the back of his hand, if only out of courtesy— no, not to you, but to the Hallowed Name you've enlisted.

Therefore, and first of all, *kill to get a name.* Network. Ask. Throw dignity to the wind.

Once upon a time I knew a fellow who knew a fellow who'd met a Gorgeously Droppable Name—only once, at a Hamptons party— and who'd overheard the Name mumbling something to the effect that X-Y was a great company. My friend, wanting a job, began his letter:

Dear Mr. X: Droppable Name said you do the best production in town... and then launched his pitch for a job.

Or in other words, a Name by any other name is a Name, and since the Name is the name of the game, get it any whichway you can. But use caution and don't lie (as the fellow I know didn't— what he said was the literal truth. He just didn't mention that the story was thirdhand).

Scenario #2:

There isn't an opening but you still have a Name.

Dear Mr. X: Droppable Name suggested that I send you a resumé...

Scenario #3:

The cold solicitation. You aren't sure there's a job, and you haven't got a connection:

Dear Mr. X: I read that you just got the Trivial account. I'm a sales rep with six years of trivial experience, and on the chance that you're hiring, I'm enclosing a resumé.

Dear Mr. X: I'm a cost accountant working at Stooge & Legree but I'd rather work for you.

Dear Mr. X: If you're looking for a draftsman with aeronautic experience, I'm enclosing a resumé, and hope you'll keep me in mind.

SCENARIO #4:

You don't have experience. Or you do but it's not related.

Lead with your best shot and, if you've nothing stunning to offer, offer to work hard. And show you've considered Them.

Dear Mr. X: I'm a graduate (cum laude) of Fine University where I majored in English, minored in History, and aimed to make a career in nonfiction publishing. Specifically, I've always admired [Your Company] for the depth and breadth of its lists, the quality of its editing and the chances it likes to take. I can offer you energy, a lot of enthusiasm, a willingness to learn and to work long and hard at any and all beginner's assignments.

Dear Mr. X: I've just returned from active duty in Iraq...

¶ The "I've Got a Project" Letter

You want to sell a free-lance project or service. The rules are roughly the same. Get a name, drop it first. Beyond that, the letter itself should be short, with a short, to-the-heart-of-it summary of your project, with the details in a (short) presentation to be attached.[4] The rest of your letter may include your credentials, the selling points of your [whatsis], or its benefits to your reader. Again, don't hallucinate. Stocking your first novel will not be of notable benefit to Amazon; but buying your services

4 Unsolicited presentations should be shorter than 4 pages—double-spaced and easy to read (and see the chapter on Presentations). If you've got a brochure, send it. If you're selling something that's graphic— like a landscaping or interior decorating service, or one-of-a-kind necklaces or one-of-a-kind cakes —then a photo or two is fine. But if you can't pitch coherently in 4 pages or fewer, just tantalize in your letter. A letter with those intentions is officially known as a "query": you're pitching the broad outlines and politely asking your reader if he'd like to listen to more..

of teaching ESL to production-line workers might actually be a boon to a company making boats.

¶ The "Follow-up" Letter

Following an interview. Following a meeting. Following a job you (or they) have completed. Following a favor either you or they did. And last, but most horrible, following the prospectus or the resumé you sent to which you never got an answer. Or following the question to which you never got an answer. Each of them has a function.

The follow-up to an interview, at least if it went well, is the easiest one to write. You "really enjoyed meeting" them. Something they said was "helpful." Or it gave you a further thought, which you can now (quickly) express. Is there something you neglected to impart in the interview that might help your case? Is there something unrelated that was mentioned during the interview? (Your mutual love of cats?) If you're clever enough and subtle enough, drag in the cat.

About that cat: Often, in any kind of tenuous correspondence, what you're looking for is a pretext— an excuse to write a letter. The actual point of the letter is just "Please remember my name," "please note that I'm well-mannered," and "listen, I liked you too." (Even bosses are human beings, and human beings like to be liked.) A follow-up letter, provided it's properly tuned, offers an edge on the competition.

The follow-up to a meeting where business has been discussed with a new or prospective client can again refer to your pleasure at the wonders of having met them, can again praise their wisdom, or respond to a floating question or invite them to ask others. It can also recapitulate whatever you think happened (like instructions you think you were given, or the things you agreed to do). This can serve as a written record (both for them, you, and His Honor) and precludes some recriminations.

The follow-up letter at the end of a job you'd done is a warm "it was great to work with you," along with a reassurance that you're not dropping them cold. If they have a remaining question, you'll be more than glad to respond. If it was they who performed the service, note your special appreciation, as you'd do if they'd done you a favor. Every favor deserves a thanks.

On the other end of the rainbow—on the end with the Wicked Witch where they sadistically torture Toto— there's the letter of "Thanks for nothing" which is more like a "Dunning Letter," and even more like a stifled scream. When they've never answered your questions, when they've never returned your samples, when they've neatly ignored your perfectly wonderful letter, letters or call(s) and when you still need to get [whatever], you can't avoid it, you have to write, and the only question remains, How?

First: hold your temper. It could take a muzzle and leash, but just hold it. Hold also any hint of whimper or whine and save your outrage for City Hall. Venting may feel delicious but it rarely gets what you want.

Dear Mr. X: My letter might easily have slipped through the cracks, but I wrote you last August inquiring about...

Dear Mr. X: I do hate to bother you again with this matter but [the barn's still on fire] and [I'm still waiting for water].

When you're finally out of patience, put the ball in your own court:

Dear Mr. X: As you requested, I sent you a book of samples at the end of the 20th century, asking to have them back within the next month and a half. I'm sure that it's slipped your mind, but perhaps you could ask your assistant to have them ready by Wednesday morning when my mother will pick them up.

Suppose what you're dunning him about is a presentation. A month is a decent interval in which to expect a reply. After that, you can start to "wonder."

Dear Mr. X: Name That I Dropped Before had suggested I send you samples. I did, about a month ago, and now begin to wonder if they'd gotten lost in the mail...

The lost-in-mail gambit is a semi-reasonable pretext and elides any accusation. And your sweet, ingenuous offer to send him another set will send him scurrying through the pile because the last thing he wants to get is yet another set of your samples.

Dear Mr. X: I wondered if you've yet had a chance to take a look at my Widget Presentation...

Now rattle your own brain. To disguise the bald nag, is there any other plausible reason to write again?

...because I'm leaving for Madagascar on Monday, the 21st...

...because the offer ends in July...

...because the material is time-sensitive and I'll have to send it elsewhere by the middle of next week...

...because I've had another offer and, though I do very strongly favor Your Company, I'll have to accept it— or not— by the 21st.

Is there any other *semi*-plausible reason?

Dear Mr. X: I wondered if, along with the widget presentation, I'd mistakenly enclosed my Chihuahua, Louise...

Dear Mr. X: Yesterday, I ran into Close Mutual Friend who informed me that you'd won the Nobel in economics and I wanted to say "Yo!"

Okay. Let us reason here quietly together. Let us, if we can, fathom your reader's mind.

Why Hasn't He Answered?

Since psychology is part of your business-writing arsenal, it helps if you understand.

A: He didn't like it (whatever it is you sent) and universally, people are chicken. They detest confrontations. They abhor turning you down and having to deal with your disappointment or your efforts to change their minds. Further, and too often, they're inclined to take the position that if you're not worth hiring, you're not worth answering.

B: He hasn't read it.

I. And won't ever, regardless of what you do.

II. Will eventually, but not till there's ice in hell.

III. Could be encouraged to if charmingly re-approached. (Squeaky wheels getting oil.)

Okay, in his defense, like every other executive, he's right up to his comb-over in unsolicited mail. He's also loaded with work, or *believes* he's loaded with work, which comes down to the same thing. If he can find a moment to spare, he wants to spend it grabbing a smoke or that insatiable girl in Accounting. Then, too, he's got what he needs. He's got adequate suppliers that he's used for the last decade, and several other projects that are still warming the shelf. And even if he's nuts about whatever it is you're pitching, he'd rather avoid the risk. (You could prove to be unreliable; your project could be a dud.) Saying No costs him nothing. Not reading it at all doesn't even cost him an hour.

C. He's read it and he actually likes it but he has to go to the Board. Or to seven other Departments. And *they* haven't read it. Which puts him in approximately the same position as you— needing to (and similarly, hating to) follow up. The reason he hasn't responded is: he doesn't want to admit that he's as powerless as he is, or, more generously interpreted, he doesn't want to lift you up and then slap you down in case the rest of the gang hates it. So he hopes to avoid contact till he's ready for yes or no — and if it happens to be a no, he'll...hope to avoid contact. (See A, up above.)

True, you can never know which of these applies to your own particular case, but you can try to cover some bases.

Reassurance— which also reminds him of your existence— might possibly do the trick. Or not, but it's worth a try:

Dear Mr. X: I recently sent you a widget proposal. It occurred to me I hadn't sufficiently spelled out...

And then sweeten the pot as you will—

...that I've never, in the course of my career, missed a deadline and I never over-promise. When I estimate a job will take two weeks to do, it'll be done in two weeks...

...that the first month is free...

...that not only has my company worked with The Big Deal, but you can reach Mr. Deal at [telephone number] if you'd like to check us out.

Suppose that you've already written your second letter and you still haven't heard a word. You've called and he's "out of town" or even worse "on the other line." The question is, when should you consider letting it drop? Answer: it's up to you. If the person you're pitching to is the only person to pitch (or else one of a very few) then you may have nothing to lose. If it's already No, then it's already No, and at least you'll know for sure. And maybe it's a Maybe. And maybe your third letter will remind him to read your first.

If you're creative, be creative (to the extent the traffic will bear).

Someone I once knew had collected a bunch of blank picture post-cards from many ports. Everywhere from Thailand to Disneyland to the Alps—and sent one of them, once a week:

Dear Mr. X: Bali's magnificent. Have you read my pitch?

Dear Mr. X: Wish you were here but as long as you're still there... have you read my pitch?

(No, I'm not advising it, but it did happen to work.)

Here's something I myself once did that I thought tacky though it actually did the trick:

Dear Mr. X: I really do want to do [Name of Presentation] which is why I'm not taking no answer for an answer. So how about a quick one. (Check one and return.)

__ *I never got your presentation. Please send a copy.*

__ *I got it but I've been too busy to read it.*

__ *I read it but I didn't like it.*

__ *I liked it but everyone <u>else</u> has been too busy to read it.*

__ *Everyone else read it and it's under consideration and we'll let you know by ______________.*

__ *Everyone else read it and <u>nobody</u> liked it.*

__ *Other: ____________________________________.*

The guy, to my tremendous relief, found it funny and he called me the next day. And I eventually got the deal.

Caution: Keep in mind that this particular wacky letter was aimed at a known guy with a particular sense of humor. I can offer it as a model, but consider doing it "straight" unless you're very sure of your reader.

The main point, however, is, you *should* follow up. If they're never going to read it and never going to answer, then you've really nothing to lose. And remember, if you can, the Godfather's consolation: "It's not personal, it's just business."

¶ <u>The Letter of Apology</u>

Begin with the bottom line. "I'm genuinely sorry" "I'm so very sorry," "I truly regret," "I deeply apologize" or, depending on the context as well as on the reader, "Boy, did I blow it." If your frankly-confessed error cost somebody else money, offer to reimburse him. Or ask what you can do to make it better or clean it up. Or *suggest* what you can do to make it better or clean it up. If you have an excuse give it, but allow that it's "no excuse." This buttery-mouthed approach, of course, presumes that you're really guilty (or at least arguably so).

But what happens when you're not?

What happens when your customer ordered the red sofa... and now complains that it's red? Or when you're blasted for not following the instructions you weren't given, or for anything else on earth that has your reader in high dudgeon without a shred of probable cause?

Answer: Apologize. Not for your actions, but your customer's disappointment, or the reigning "misunderstanding."

Dear Mrs. X: We're genuinely sorry you're disappointed with the sofa. Even though as you'll see on your order form (enclosed) that you did order red, we can offer to accommodate you in one of the three ways that are listed on your contract...

Dear Mr. X: I can understand your anger at being, as you say, "stuck with a useless fern," but I can only assure you it was based on a misunderstanding. While Ms. Moronic appears convinced that she gave us the new instructions, we're quite equally convinced that those instructions were never given, but it's water over the dam and your problem remains unsolved, so I'd like to propose a solution.

¶ The Letter of Complaint

Actually I think this was somewhat covered above. If you're hoping for Satisfaction, hold your temper and stick to facts. Never use a word you wouldn't use to your sainted mother. Never wish a Horrible Fate to befall your perp. Begin with the crux of the problem. List all of the pertinent facts and only the pertinent facts. State soberly what happened. State soberly what you want, and *exactly* what you want. Give an exact deadline— and after it's been ignored, threaten nothing except a lawsuit.

¶ The Dunning Letter

Your invoice hasn't been paid. The whatever-it-is-you-hired-them-for either hasn't been done or is well past deadline. Yes, you're apoplectic but the same rules apply: Never get abusive. Always allow your welsher a chance to save face. Your goal, please remember, is to get whatever you want. In other words:

The Money.

After 30 —or 60 or 90— days have passed, your impulse will be to phone, but use the telephone with caution. A small business or, even more so, a private individual will likely avoid your call. Or the conversation itself can turn eruptive or maudlin and in many cases leave you more stumped than you were before. On the other hand, if you're dealing with a major corporate labyrinth, you can shyly approach Billing— a rabbit warren remote from the executives you've dealt with— and try to straighten it out. Or, depending on the circumstances, yes, call the executive and try to enlist his help. After *that*, when nothing happens, you can always resort to mail.

Okay, what to mail? For openers, you can start with your original invoice, its original date circled. If it's simply going to Billing, write "Duplicate" "Overdue," and add a handwritten epilogue. Something along the lines of "We'd appreciate your payment." If you're dealing with The Executive, send him the second invoice but along with a covering note:

Dear Jack: As you can see, the accountants haven't paid me. Can you see what's holding them up and apply a little pressure? I'll call you next Monday in search of a Later Bulletin.

Even if Jack himself is the blackguard who's holding it up, don't treat him as The Enemy, treat him as The Friend.

Of course it's always nice if you can hold something for ransom.

Dear Jack: As you can see, the accountants haven't paid me for the first seven commandments. Unhappily, I can't deliver the next three until I receive a check.

Let's see if we can formulate a practical generalization— an all purpose model for escalated dunning. The usual opening anodyne is something along the lines of "perhaps you've overlooked..." and goes on to "appreciate" immediate payment. The next letter is civil though it flexes a little muscle, reminding your debtor that (much to your own regret) interest will start to accumulate or service will be suspended as of [very specific date], which you're sure he'll want to avoid. Your third letter is tough (interest has been accruing; service has been suspended) but still offers a bone. If he'd like to make arrangements to pay you out over time, you'll be happy to accommodate and work with him on a schedule. Your final letter refers to "attorneys, "collectors," or the furies of Judge Judy.

Suppose, on the other hand, you're merely a free-lancer and you've nothing to hold for ransom, not even your future service. Your work is already done and, even worse, in their grubby hands.

Still, your first letter is a civil statement of fact. They agreed to pay you $X,000 by April 1st and it's now past Arbor Day. Please, would they give this their immediate attention. Your next letter expresses a sense of your shocked surprise. They were such honorable people! You find it hard to believe that they'd purposely dodge a debt. Can they offer an explanation along with a plan to pay? *No?* Grab a lever. If you can— realistically— threaten them with a lawsuit to prevent their using your stuff. And finally, once again, you've got the bludgeon of "my attorney" and the hint of a warm subpoena to respond in a "court of law." [5]

If you're dealing with a private individual or customer and you're not really close enough for "Harriet, What's up?" but you're not quite remote enough for "Have you overlooked…?":

Dear Mrs. X: Just to let you know that your check for the photographs still hasn't arrived. If you sent it a while ago, you might want to stop payment and issue another check…

If you unluckily took the photos for your brother-in-law's cousin, it can obviously get sticky and can lead to a family fued. But, yes, if he sends you nothing, you can still take him to court, though your brother-in-law may never let you play with his toys again and your sister may French your bed. However, if you sue— either him or anyone else— you'll still, for the legal record, have to tell him of your intent:

5 Even without an "attorney," you can still take them to court. Check the rules for your own city in the matter of Small Claims..

Dear Robert: This is getting either serious or silly. You haven't answered my letters and you haven't sent me a check. If I don't get your payment for the full amount you owe me by Monday the 23rd, I'll be forced to take it to court.

And then...take it to court. Or to put that another way, don't threaten idly.

Aside from the bailiwick of Unanswered Questions (see The Follow-up Letter) the other reason to dun involves:

Overdue Work.

Of course, you can always just fire the wretched slouch but it's not always convenient. He's holding your down payment. Half the job is already done. There isn't time to begin anew. Or he's your brother-in-law's cousin. Again, your first letter gives him cover to save his face and appeals to a Better Nature you're increasingly sure he lacks.

Dear Mr. Messup: As you know, we'd agreed that the Ark would be built by June before the flood season arrives, and I know from your reputation that you'll surely honor your word. Still, if you're having problems in completing the forward hull, would you let me know what they are so we can possibly work around them.

Your next letter *demands.* He either does it by [date certain] or [threaten him as you will]. Your final letter's the Kiss-off, with a follow-through on your threats.

¶ The White Rabbit Letter

You're late. You've blown— or you're deeply into the process of blowing— a deadline, or your payment is overdue. Recalling the Golden Rule, it's up to *you* to write *them.* Apologize first. Keep your list of excuses short (and as poignant as you can make them), and immediately offer a plan. You can pay them off in installments of [$100 a week], or all at once in [another month]. You can hand in the missing work by [whatever date you can do it] or suggest a replacement worker. Your honor is on the line. And so is your reputation. Don't chicken out on this. Write it. Write it now.

¶ The Dear John Letter

This is not quite the Kiss-off; this is more of a soft let-down. You're letting somebody go, you're dispensing with somebody's service, or you're not renewing a contract (from either side of the fence). It's nothing they've done wrong— or nothing that it wouldn't be gratuitous to mention— it's just that... [whatever]. If you do have a reason that would help them to understand, or to feel a bit better, by all means give it. (You can no longer afford it. Or you no longer need it. Or the new agent you're going with has contacts in Pyongyang, and besides, you're expecting twins.)

Dear Sally: This has been a very difficult decision but...

Dear Harry: I'm really so sorry to have to tell you...

Similarly, if somebody's sent you a pitch or resumé that's either not what you want or else verging on the pathetic, keep in mind that, nevertheless, it was sent by a human being— a human being with real talent or a person with "hopes and dreams" and a nice mom and a fluffy dog. If you can possibly answer, answer— as kindly and, if moved to, as helpfully as you can.

¶ **The Letter You Never Send**

Sooner or later in the course of a long career someone will just enrage you. They'll tell you they hate your work or your attitude or your ears. They'll ask you to change your work or they'll change it without asking. They'll suddenly change the ground rules or, even more maddeningly, change them again and again. Or they'll simply, totally lie.

Your impulse will be to blast them with a long angry letter in which you explain exactly what a pig/ clod/ cur/ jerk/ cretin you think they are. Further, you'll want to explain to them, precisely and point by point, why you had to do what you did or why you couldn't do what you didn't, or why you certainly can't do what they now have the gall to ask. Further, you'll want to recount to them with near-psychotic precision the entire historical record: what they promised, and when they said, and then you told them, and how they sneezed.

Great. Do it. Get the fury out of your system. (And while you're busy elaborating on why their instructions stink, you may actually find a solution. Perhaps with some minor changes, you could actually make it work.) But whatever you do with your letter, do not—*not*— send it. (And never flirt with temptation by proceding on blank email; your finger, without permission, can triumphantly hit "send" and you'll be sending the wrong message.)

Leave your letter. Leave it alone. Let it marinate overnight while you stew in a separate corner. "What," you may ask yourself while gnawing an errant cuticle, "would presumably be my goal?" "And what," you may ask yourself while stomping a hapless water bug, "would actually be at stake?" Would you, by sending it, tarnish your reputation? Lose contacts or opportunities? Or major amounts of money? If so, do you really care? And even if you don't, will a tirade add to your case? Or else, in a game of Gotcha, will it merely prove you were got?

Try your letter again in the morning when the high ground is better attained. [6]

¶ **The Kiss-Off.**

Let it fly. You've got nothing further to lose. Fire them, quit them, accuse them of what they did. Document your grievances (as long as they're provably real) and give vent to your full outrage. BUT— watch your language. Keep it classy and keep it clean. Say nothing you couldn't prove before the highest court in the land. Say nothing that would make you seem ridiculous, petty or nuts. Say nothing that smacks vaguely of a whimpering "poor me" or a whiney "look how you've hurt me." This is business; stick to the facts. And never, never, never mail a kiss-off the same day. As with Letters You Never Send, let it cool by an open window, over the weekend, or overnight, and then shred it and write it coolly in the glare of a cold light.

---

6 Or perhaps, in the tiny hours, an inspiration will kiss your brow. I recall a vivid occasion where a magazine editor had so distorted my work that it wound up expressing things I violently disagreed with. First, I wrote The Letter, dissecting, line by line, the intrusion of her atrocities, demanding they all be changed. After all, it was *my column;* after all it was *my name.* After several fuming hours, I was cooled by a realization: after all, it was *her magazine!*. Second of all, I hadn't a contractual leg stand on (they didn't "owe" me the changes) and even were the editor delighted to eat crow (a truly dubious proposition) there physically wasn't time (the magazine had to go to press) so my effusions would get me nothing. The solution then— at 4 o'clock in the morning— became a breeze. Don't ask them to change the article, demand that they change the byline. And lo! this was accomplished in the course of a three-line note. Everybody was happy. The editor got her article, I got to save my name, and I never— by volition— worked for the rag again.

9.
RESUMÉS

A resumé means "a summary." Its slightly affected synonym, "curriculum vitae,"[1] which is Latin for "course of life," is exactly the same thing except in Latin instead of French, and in either case refers to what you're doing and what you've done and where you did it and how you learned. The challenge of writing resumés is not inconsiderable. It requires, among other things, a search for the right format (a running order that points up your assets and hides your flaws), an eye for the telling detail, an ear for the proper tone, and the discipline to ruthlessly reduce to a single page the irreducible facts of a lifetime.

The operative word is "facts."

RULE: NEVER NEVER LIE ABOUT YOUR EXPERIENCE.

Morality aside— and it should never be put aside— it's just flat-out stupid. Too many crooks have already spoiled the broth. By now, so many people have lied on their resumés that employers now check you on everything you've said. And getting caught in a lie will do you much more (serious, irreparable) harm than the lie you concocted could have ever done you good.

Beginners (and even middlers who are switching to new tracks) will undoubtedly beat their brains against Catch-22:

**YOU CAN'T GET EXPERIENCE
IF YOU DON'T HAVE EXPERIENCE,
AND YOU CAN'T HAVE EXPERIENCE
IF YOU CAN'T EVER GET IT.**

That particular conundrum is older than old hills. Everybody work-

---

1 Though they're often (mis)used as synonyms, a curriculum vitae differs from a resumé in that it's meant to apply to academics and other specialists such as scientists and doctors. A true C.V. can be several pages long because it frequently has to specify the titles of published papers and the details of major projects. When you use it to mean resumé, it makes you look pretentious.

ing in America today has had to stumble his way around it but it's always and forever conquered the same way: with talent, energy, persistence, and good luck.

You have absolutely *no* control over your luck and only partial control of your talent, but the two things that do rest entirely in your hands are your resolve and determination. In order to eventually do what you want to do, you'll have to do what you have to do: Work hard. Apprentice. Sweat. Bust your tail. Make everything you do the very best you can do and then do it another mile.

And all that together doesn't get you a guarantee. Luck, good or bad, will play a definite and fairly major part in your career. Don't believe automatically that when and if you've succeeded it was simply because you're brilliant, or that when and if you failed it was simply because you're not. Nobody's ever nailed it quite as nakedly as the Bible:

And I saw that under the sun the race is not to the swift,
nor the battle to the strong, nor bread to the wise,
nor prizes to the intelligent, nor favor to men of skill,
but time and chance do happen to them all.

You bear total responsibility for everything you do, but no responsibility for the doings of time and chance. The only thing you can do to lay bait for their feckless fancies is to ready yourself for their knock by attempting to be as swift, strong, wise, smart and skilled as your dedication can take you. After that, it's up to Them.

But if *They* haven't handed you a bucket of opportunities (and yes, they do hand them to a couple of lucky souls), then you'll simply have to create them. So, too, with experience. If you don't have it, create it.

I don't mean fabricate it; I mean create it.

Create it in your school, create it in your office, create it in your community. Be willing to work for nothing except the experience. Do speculative projects. Do anything remotely related to your goals. Enter contests. Try for grants. Join groups that offer contacts and professional affiliations: guilds, societies, workshops, clubs. And show up at their meetings. Serve on their committees, contribute to their projects. Everything you do can be grist for your resumé. Or else, look at it this way: If you don't intrinsically enjoy what you're doing, then... why would you want to do it?

The second, more tractable part of a good resumé is... a good resumé. And now we're talking technically (getting the right format) as well as strategically (doing the right sell).

The best way to start undertaking a resumé is simply to understand what a resumé is, which is possibly best explained by—

WHAT A RESUME ISN'T.

1. A resumé is not an ad:

INTRODUCING THE NEW IMPROVED KAREN SMITH
THE PLANET'S MOST TALENTED COMPUTER PROGRAMMER
(Now Available at 20% off!)

It contains no puffery, no vanity, no sell. (It "sells," all right, but it sells without selling.)

2. A resumé is not an autobiography.

It shouldn't be written in the first person ("I") nor, for that matter, in the third person ("he") and certainly never in the editorial "we". Nor does it recount every breath of your life, or even every breath of your previous career.

3. A resumé is not an inspirational tract.

It should not be filled with inspirational clichés like "I thrive on challenges," "my ambition is for excellence," lines that sound faintly as though they came from your monthly horoscope, and certainly lines that would never come out of your mouth. Resumés, in fact, should never be filled with *lines*, but simply with hard facts.

4. A resumé is not a personals ad

It does not include items like SWF.[2] Your age, race, faith, weight, marital status and hobbies (trail hiking, scuba diving, classical music) are entirely irrelevant— unless you're applying for a job as a park ranger, a Key West tour guide, or an opera critic.

And please, may I beg of you, spare me the self-descriptives.

---

2 In fact, listing any of your vitaler statistics may work to your disadvantage on the grounds (get this) that they compromise a boss's oath to avoid bias, and thus, in the name of Tolerance, can force him to count you out.

Personally when I come upon an adjective-laden resumé (*dynamic results-centered business-savvy professional*) I mentally start to add *seeks adaptable blonde companion for dinners, theater and cuddles.* Nor is my irreverence entirely off the mark. You may, for all I know, be dynamic, savvy and swell, but the trouble is we're living in an age with enough hype to turn a guppy into a cynic, and the top-of-the-head response to such effusions is "Sez who?" Once again, many gurus will instruct you in this bravado, but my own approach to it is, let the facts speak for themselves. If you've worked as a Mob Enforcer, I'll assume that you're quick and bold. What I really want to know is what you *did* as a Mob Enforcer.

What a resumé *is*, then, as far as I'm concerned, is simply and tersely an outline of what you did. It exists to tell potential employers *at a glance:*

¶ Your abilities

¶ Your accomplishments

¶ Your experience (where? when?)

¶ Your training (where? when?)

¶ And how these relate to whatever the job at hand.

Period. That's it. If your resumé speaks about your character and ambitions, it speaks between the lines, and only between the lines. *On* the lines, it deals with the concrete specifics.

Your goal, in creating it, is to choose the right specifics, and present them in the savviest order and best light.

But note: order-and-light tends to vary with time and tide. In fact, it may vary from one application-for-a-job to another— even if you're applying for both on the same day. Employer #1 wants a chef for his "high-volume, full service restaurant that's centered around sports." Employer #2 wants a chef for his "upscale wedding facility." All *you* want is a job. But perhaps the same resumé won't work for both. Yes, you'll be dealing with the same set of (true) biographical facts, but the order you put them in and which ones you stress, the details you mention and which you leave out may indeed make the difference in netting you the job(s). Then, too, if you're right now working as a programmer and you're looking for a *better* job as a programmer, but you'd secretly like to work as a landscape designer (your lifelong ambition) then you'd probably want to give yourself two (or more) resumés, one for each goal.

Fortunately, technology has made this a snap. Gone are the days when The Resumé was something that had to be mass produced. Your computer now allows you the singular advantage of the custom-made, handmade, I-am-as-you-desire-me, professional-looking, strategized and streamlined response.

How to go about it is the subject of this chapter. But before we get deeply into strategy and choice, let's first do the easy part:

THE TECHNICAL PART

Let's start with the fact that while there's no magic formula, no single, guaranteed way to do it right, there are several guaranteed ways to do it wrong, so let's start by avoiding them. In general, the hard-and-fast rules remain these:

First, keep it brief. Resumés should never (or at least hardly ever) be longer than one page. If you're vastly experienced, with numerous, varied and prestigious accomplishments— 30 or 40 years worth of knock-out credentials— you could go to a second page, but never— even if you're God— more than two.

Come to think of it, even God could do it in one page:

> *Created the universe and everything in it; continue to supervise all the above. (c. 4 billion BC to present.)*

If you *don't* have a long list of wowing experience, padding and puffery won't help your case.

And whatever your experience, too many details can undercut your strengths and distract from what's important. (If you designed and executed the Sistine ceiling, you don't have to add that you also once dabbled in hand-painted shoes.) Know what's important. Knowing what's important is a talent in itself— which is why I've been nudging you to "get to the essence."

Keeping it brief means your sentences, too. A resumé is more like a list than an essay. Phrases, instead of whole sentences, will do. Eliminate pronouns (the "I" is implicit). Eliminate adjectives, adverbs and even— where it's possible— verbs.

Second, make it perfect. Start with good paper, preferably with paper that matches your stationary. Next, understand that your type has to be crisp and your text has to be perfect— no typos, no left out or careted-in words, and zero misspellings. Proofread carefully. Then proofread again. Then leave it overnight and... proofread again.

Further, make sure that within the selected format, your layout is pleasing and encouraging to the eye, with judiciously used white space (the text blocks of resumés are always single- spaced) and judiciously used bullets.

Finally: stick to a proper format. And note I said "a" since there's no one format that will work for the whole world. But one thing's for certain: there's a logic to resumés; the trick is to find the right logic that works for yours.

Still, before we wander about vaguely to far fields, let's talk about:

THE RUNNING ORDER OF A RÉSUME.

A. THE BEGINNING

It's generally acknowledged that, at least in the first go-round, employers glance at resumés for 15 to 30 seconds. Yes, I said seconds. Obviously, you need to communicate *fast*. The "experts," however, inconveniently disagree on what— exactly— to communicate *first*. I'll summarize their thoughts and then throw in my own nickel.

1. Who are you?

No disagreement. The first four items are your letterhead items (and, ideally, you'll want to do them in your letterhead font): your name, address, telephone number(s) and email.

2. What do you do? *OR* What do you want to do?

The experts start to tangle on the second order of business. In general, I vote for the simple "What do you do?" A no-frills statement of your current, or at least of your major, occupation.

Administrative Assistant
Menswear Buyer
Editor-in-chief

Others believe the second item on your resumé should be your objective or, to put that another way:

Objective: Editor, financial publication
Job Objective: Senior-level marketing position

On the other hand, your goals might belong in your covering letter, and will usually be implicit. If you're right now [an editor], if you're answering a want ad they placed for [an editor], if you're mailing it all off to a [financial magazine], they'll undoubtedly figure it out. And meanwhile, your resumé, by not starting blatantly with *Listen, I need a job*, looks cooler and less supplicant— always a good idea.

On the *other* Other Hand, there are three situations where it actually makes sense to confide your objectives.

: If you're looking for (and only for) a specialized position:

Objective: To work as a mechanical engineer in applied R & D for medical devices

: If you're looking for advancement—and only advancement— and would not consider moving to a job at your present level, even for more money. For example, you're an editorial assistant and you want to become an editor.

Objective: Editor, trade fiction

: If you're just starting out (a recent graduate) or you want to change careers. You're a broadcasting major and you want to be an anchor. You're a secretary in a box factory and you want to be an FM radio disc jockey. In which case, you might make the modest proposal:

Objective: To work in broadcasting.

Stating a relatively modest objective will give you a better shot at getting *some* kind of starting position at the station, from which, with application, good taste and a sexy voice, you might work your way up.

On the first Other Hand, stating an objective is so frequently recommended for any and all resumés that I'm offering you the option, but I caution you: keep it simple.

Wrong:

JOB OBJECTIVE: To advance, grow, and conquer the upcoming challenges in 21st century laundry.

Right:

JOB OBJECTIVE: Manager, launderette.

3. What's the general range of your expertise?

Next, at least optionally, you can, if you like, give a resumé of your resumé— a thumbnail summation of the substance of your career. You can do it in a paragraph, or do it with bullets:

SENIOR MARKETING ANALYST

Ten years' experience with major corporations creating strategies and analyzing trends in home furnishings, automotive, electronics and fine art. Efforts have resulted in market share growth (up to 97%) and rise in productivity (up to 78%). Additional experience in managing large staffs.

EXECUTIVE ASSISTANT

: *Right hand to Senior Executives in healthcare and financial industries.*
: *Acted as liaison to—and between—30 branch offices.*
: *Coordinated major national projects.*
: *Wrote progress reports for upper management.*
: *Additional skills: Office procedures; Database management; Powerpoint, Excel, MS Office, Star8.*

Note: Absolutely no bloviation (no *excellent, superior, dedicated, dynamic*), and not so much as a breath about *results-orientation*, or any other buzz words of banal bureaucratese. The facts speak for themselves. (A guy who doubled the sales is implictly no slouch. And implicitly, any woman who could juggle with 30 branches and coordinate a *pizza*, never mind an important project, is a jewel beyond compare.) [3]

---

3 Again, many experts will instruct you in bloviation and offer you the Top Ten Adjectives of the Week. Go along with them if you will. They're all over the internet and featured in many books. Compare, contrast, and then ultimately decide.

Rank beginners can play too. Begin with your education and proceed to the kitchen sink (naming only the hot faucets).

MFA, CINEMAPHOTOGRAPHY/ BA, ART HISTORY
¶ Master's degree: NYU Tisch School of the Arts
¶ Gluten Award Winner 2007 (short documentary)
¶ Summertime intern:
Museum of Modern Art; WNET (PBS), New York
¶ "Gallery Scene" column for The CUNY Courier
¶ Online reviews for The Curve and The Village Voice
¶ Group show exhibits (photography/ animation)
¶ Photoshop, After Effects, Cinema4D, Final Cut, & more

This thumbnail, however, while an excellent way to start, isn't always the way to start. In other words, it's a judgment call and you is duh judge.

B. The Middle

For the middle point on, the patterns of organization and their plausible variations begin to adopt the form of a multiple choice question in which all answers are right (but only right some of the time). What follows are the three most commonly used formats. Be aware, however, that employers— or, at least, most corporate employers— will vastly favor the first.

I. Chronological (In Reverse)

The next item on deck in the most conventional format takes you straight into HISTORY, also known as EXPERIENCE, also known as WORK or PROFESSIONAL EXPERIENCE, or don't even title it and simply plunge in. Titled or not, in a chronological resumé, a list and a brief explanation of your jobs should be the third or fourth item. Begin by listing when and where you did what— beginning with right now and going backward to days of yore. The details to be included are:

The name of the company, the city (if it's different from the city you're in now), the title of your job, your customary duties, your major accomplishments, the dates of your employment.

All of these should be listed briefly and selectively. By which I mean, first of all:

Don't state the obvious.

If you're a shoe salesman, your reader expects that you "sold shoes." So what else did you do lately that he might *not* expect? Were you responsible for weekly inventory checks? Did you sub for the branch manager? Dress the front windows? *Un*dress in the front windows as a way to increase sales?

Be selective about details.

Do Step Two thinking. Summarize. Generalize. You're a medical secretary. Your duties consisted of [X, Y and Z] but the opening generalization is, "Experienced in all aspects of medical office procedure." Okay— and what else? Are you a demon typist? A master of all software? A wizard of all claim forms? List them, by all means ("90 wpm," "Quickbooks/ Excel..."). Are you happy to work with people? Are you fluent in Japanese? Are you willing to work weekends? Can you wheedle an authorization from the claws of an HMO? These are totally "telling" details and the kind that you'd want to tell. Details you *shouldn't* tell would be— just for example— "responsible for opening the office in the morning," which merely proves you know how to operate a door.

Know when enough's enough.

If, as a copywriter, you've worked on 50 accounts, don't list 50 accounts. A couple of useful phrases are a) "including" and b) "among others." You might want to specify you worked on "50 accounts, including" [and offer up the six most sexy]. You might want to indicate the range of those accounts: "food, fashion, pharmaceuticals, automotive." If you've won a dozen awards, consider "among a dozen award-winning commericials: Geico "Gecko," Mastercard "Priceless," Nexium "Burp."

Don't get compulsive.

Selectivity can also apply to the jobs you list. If, just for example, in 1996 you had a job for a couple of months that you hated and then quit (or hated and got canned), *you don't have to list it.*

A SENSIBLE OMISSION IS NOT THE SAME AS A LIE.

Similarly, too, if you're a middle-aged executive and you've spent the last several decades as an executive, you don't have to cop to all your first ragged jobs ("Mailroom, McDonald's; Sales, Sam Goody.") A *relevant* first job (you're an Allstate executive who began rather tenuously in a Met Life office) can be listed without details:

MET-LIFE INSURANCE, Saratoga, NY. (1987-1989)
: Administrative Assistant

It indicates unwavering interest in the field, accounts for a chunk of time, and presumably indicates you worked your way up, presumably through charm, dedication and good looks.

And along the same lines, if you're applying for, let's say, a job as a company spokesman, your experiences in acting might indicate to some that you've a talent for public speaking.

ACTRESS: Summer Stock, Provincetown, MA (1997-1999)
: Roles included: Kate ("Kiss Me, Kate"), Nellie ("South Pacific"), Iago ("Othello")

Below are a few examples of the details you might include as you're talking about your history:

Editor-in-Chief

WORLD'S BEST MAGAZINE (2005-present)

: Refocussed editorial philosophy and content to appeal to a younger and hipper demographic
: Hired and directed superb new design team to update the look
: Streamlined production: lead time to pub date cut by 30 days to keep content up-to-the-minute

RESULTS

: Increased circulation by 700,000
: Increased ad revenues by $1.6 M

Features Editor

SECOND BEST, INC. (2000-2005)

: Now pick the 4 or 5 best or most typical things that you did, and what you accomplished.
: Additional skills or realms of expertise

Repeat this formula going back to your first job. Omit the inessential. Or to put that another way, know what's essential. For instance, if you're currently a National Director and your job before that was a Regional Director, how telling are the details of your two earlier jobs? Could they simply be listed by date, place and title? Unless you (once again!) increased sales by 90%, or sold a totally different product, what's the purpose of droning on? If you also "managed the files" at Downe & Durty in '97, is it really relevant now? Will anyone ever pester you to "manage the files" again? Is this a skill of any importance? Apply the same logic to all your previous jobs. Too many details will simply clutter the path. Use only the details that notably add luster and are obviously relevant to the job you're approaching now. (Another good reason for a custom-made resumé.)

A beginner's resumé will follow the same pattern but can wander farther afield. For instance, list any and all jobs that you've ever held— part-time, summer or selflessly volunteer, and in this case, list them no matter how irrelevant. They indicate to employers that you know how to hold a job, have the virtues to do so, and have a basic, if worm's-eye, knowledge about business.

About Dates Of Employment

Include them wherever you can. Their absence will invite a lot of dark speculation. That you're 90 years old. Or haven't worked in a decade. That you've never held a job for more than two weeks running. That you did a turn in jail.

True, you may actually need to hide something but if you don't, don't.

You can, however, use either layout or placement to highlight or to hide. Examples will follow.

On the other hand, suppose you really *did* do some time, or haven't worked in a decade, or you're over (someone else's idea of) "the hill."

Well... you've got a problem.

And the awful joke is that it's probably easier to land another job if you were jailed for a felony than if you've simply— and lawfully— taken off a couple of years to raise kids or survived to reach 50.

Dancing Over The Gap

Let's say you haven't worked full-time for a couple of years, which invites the assumption that you're off "the cutting edge" and you've permanently lost your scissors. (That your skills have gone rusty; that you lack the experience in the latest and greatest technologies of the trade and, considering the gap, you're out of touch with "the market.")

Your goal, then, is simply to say it isn't so, and to *show* it isn't so.

For instance, by showing that you've kept on working, though not for a weekly check. If you've worked in your own field as an Independent Contractor (a/k/a Consultant), it's a more than legitimate opener. Summarize what you did and give the names of a few clients, listed "among others." If you haven't quite precisely worked in your own field, or if you've worked as a volunteer, it's nonetheless better to account for your "lost" time and to show that it's been productive:

> *EVENTS PLANNER. Middlebury Library System.*
> *Planned and coordinated fundraising dinners*
> *and bi-monthly readings by popular writers.*
> *Arranged publicity in all media. Published,*
> *produced newsletters (iWorks)(2006-present)*

Or to show that you've kept abreast of what's "edgy" and "cutting" by recently attending seminars or classes, or something else tangible to update your skills. If so, and if you're choosing the chronological format, perhaps your top listing could be something like this:[4]

> *ADDITIONAL EDUCATION (2008-9)*
> *School of Visual Arts, New York City*
> *"Creativity for the 21st Century and Beyond"*
> *"Mac Photoshop, 15.6," "Photo-animation"*

About Ageism

If you're over 45, the second you enter the interviewer's office (unless your plastic surgeon is a lot better than most), it'll be clear that you're not 20. And you may well be looking into the bright eyes of

4 Alternatively, you could list this first under "Education.".

ageism, a prejudice as stupid and as rank as the other isms, but, alas, even more common.

The institutional rationale for perpetuating the bigotry is that workers of "certain ages" will increase the cost of insurance. The personal rationale (held by youngsters of under 40) is that everyone over 40 is washed up, humorless, parental, and out of date.

Your goal, once again, is to show it isn't so. And of course your best defense is a provable and preferably contemporary excellence.

What happens in such an interview is grist for another book, but the goal under discussion here is getting you through the door (on the wings of a good resumé). And one way to do it is by carefully honed omission. Don't list the date of your college graduation. Arbitrarily lop off your list of employers. If, for example, you held your first job from 1975 to 1986, a) don't list it, or b) consider lopping off the "1975" and noting it, instead, as "to 1986."

Obviously, there are jobs for which ageism won't apply but, unfortunately, they're rare. How you deal with it is a judgment call. The judgment's up to you.

II. Organized By Skills

This is a good format for: people with many, perhaps unrelated, skills, or with gaps in their "history" or length in their teeth. Prospective employers may interpret these assets as negative liabilities. Like "job hopper," "grifter," "felon" or "old."

Your job is to conjure up a credible resumé that disguises the fact that you're disguising the facts. One way to do it is The Skills Resumé, which, if done well, can reconfigure a job hopper into a fascinating Renaissance Man.

In this case, you're throwing chronology to the winds, and organizing your resumé around your various skills, obviously listing the most-wanted ones first (and always keeping in mind that your resumé is modular— that, depending on what you're going for, you can lead with a different skill). Dates are advised, though, if gamey, remain optional. And your actual Work History can be buried down at the bottom. So— just for example:

COMPUTER TECHNICIAN (HARDWARE/SOFTWARE; MAC/ PC)

¶ *Hands-on instruction, personal and corporate*

¶ *Trouble-shooting; Tracking glitches to source*

¶ *Installations and interfaces*

¶ *Debugging*

¶ *Repairs*

¶ *Recovery of "lost" files*

¶ *Buyers' advisor*

GRAPHICS— DESIGN AND PRODUCTION

¶ *Book design: typography, layout, production*

¶ *Work with traditional and On Demand publishers*

¶ *Titles, among others:*

: *"Mary Had a Lamb," (Crony & Dunce)*
hard cover, 370 pages, with 4C plates

: *"Time Watcher" (Borden House)*
mass market, 220 pages

: *"Ventor and Cloud" (Moribund) E-book*

HISTORY

Independent Consultant, Los Angeles
Charlie's Chop Shop, Seattle, WA
Nerds On Wheels, Seattle, WA
Apple Core, Inc, Chicago, IL

EDUCATION: *University of Chicago, BFA, 2006*

Okay; it's clear you're a sort of a grifter, but an able grifter; a problem solver; a "self-starter"; an independent thinker. Somebody somewhere will value those traits, and if not, you wouldn't much like to work for them anyway.

Keep in mind, too, that this resumé is modular. You can play around with the order. If you're going after a job as a book designer, you'll lead with design. And if that's your objective, and if this is your bio, and you want my opinion, I'd conflate the computer stuff to one brief paragraph (*Computer Tech/ Instructor*), summarize my skills (stressing the ones applicable to book designing), and entirely ditch the Where. Further, I'd design the pants off my resumé, stress my education and training in the arts and, if possible, include a good spread from one of the books.

My very own resumé, just for the record, is a Skills Resumé, not because I'm trying to deep-six a skeleton but because it makes sense. I list two occupations. The first (or the second, depending) is Writer. Under it, I subdivide my writing into slots (Business, Journalism, Television, Novels). The second (or the first, depending) is Teacher. Under it, I list what and where I've taught, when. And again, depending on what it is I'm after, I'll either elaborate fully on a subgroup (list all my novels along with their publishers) or summarize briefly. (*18 published novels, including...* and specify the three with awards.)

III. Best Foot Forward

When you've torn out sufficient clumps of your lovely hair and ruined a ream of paper and nothing has seemed to work, you can always resort to The Best Foot Forward. Open with absolutely everything you've got, combining all your accomplishments, all your qualifications, and all your myriad skills into one bang-up entry, saving the when/ where of it for somewhere around the end, perhaps mumbled in mouse type.

Indeed, what you're doing will be instantly transparent, but you may be without a choice.

Keep in mind, too, that the ultimate, all-time, super-colossal killer is –

The Custom-Made Resume

This one's targeted to one specific job. It's unusually effective as an answer to an ad where the employer has been specific about what it is he wants, or in cases where you've learned (through either happenstance or research) what the hiring company needs. Here you know exactly which projects, abilities and upshots to detail (and which you can do without).

You can custom-make a resumé in any (or all) of the foregoing formats.

C. The End

Finally, at last, we're at the bottom part of the page. And here, you've got a fine, miscellaneous menu of choices, each of which can strut all the stuff that you want to strut. The only one that's required (or, in any case, expected) is the sum of your education. Let's deal with them, however, in approximate proper order.

Additional skills. Usually, additional skills are just that: *additional* skills— unexpected talents that might (who knows?) become relevant on the job, or that otherwise speak to your rounded character. These might include fluency in a second language or special computer skills, or a talent for editing film, or adeptness at CPR. Do not, however, list any hobbies, interests or sports unless you can reasonably rationalize their relevance.

Awards/ grants/ prizes. If you've got 'em, flaunt 'em. Here you can bust chronological order and lead with your best card. List the name of the award (or the grant or the prize), who gave it to you, when (skipping "when" if it's inconvenient).

AWARDS:

Oscar (best animated short) Motion Picture Academy, 1999
"Best Bite Award," American Dental Association, 2004

Special projects/ exhibits. If, as an artist, you've been exhibited anywhere, if, as a writer, you've had a play produced anywhere (even in the grungiest community theatre) list when and where. If you've worked as a volunteer on community projects using your relevant skills, list those too.

Publications. If you've written articles for academic, trade, or consumer magazines, or written a (published) book, list title, publisher, date.

PUBLICATIONS:

"The Bible of Mortgage Banking," Money News, Ap 2008
"Travels in Kenya," Travel & Leisure, June, 2000

Biographical listings. If you're listed in *Who's Who*, or *Women in Engineering* or any other sort of professional publication, you can add it to your resumé.

Reviews of, or articles about, your work. Was a project of yours mentioned in a trade publication, your local newspaper, or *Time*

Magazine? List the article's title, the name of the publication, and the date of the issue.

Professional memberships. Names of associations, guilds, societies, unions, clubs— whatever you belong to that's related to your field. But note: *related*. Your membership in the Elks or The Polar Bear Club is strictly your own business.

Education. This one's a must and, unless you're a recent graduate, it's always the last (or else, in rare circumstances, the second to last) entry.

List all degrees in reverse chronological order— most recent one first. The school, the degree and, optionally, your major; if applicable, your honors. Usually, the date.

EDUCATION:

Brown University, MA, Marketing, 2007

Syracuse University, BA (cum laude) 2005

If you're still attending school but expecting to eventually get an honorable discharge after serving your full time, list it like this:

Barnard College, BA, 2012 (expected)

You can also list schools you attended for a while but not quite long enough to merit a degree, or relevant courses that you took for credit.

Barnard College, attended 2004-2006

Or

ADDITIONAL EDUCATION:

"Trends in Publishing," New York University, 2009

Do not list high school.

If you're young and have no work experience to speak of, but continually made the Dean's List, edited the paper, or did anything similarly astounding while in school, you can list it on your resumé. But don't if you're older. A person in his late twenties or early thirties who's still recalling the Glory Days at old Sigma U can look seriously absurd.

A final item (that's usually not warranted) is—

Personal, Miscellaneous or Biographical. Suppose you're a Big Brother, or participate in a local literacy program; suppose you were in the Olympics, or apprenticed with Donald Trump, or clerked for the Chief Justice. Anything that indicates the wide scope of your character or the range of your talents might conceivably rate a line. But not "father of three," and not personal hobbies. And, just by the way, it's better not to offer your political affiliations.

Okay; that's it. And even with entries under all the above headings, you can— with a mixture of relentless editing and imaginative layout— stick to one page.

I know. It's still daunting. But remember: The Seven Steps that you mastered in Part One are primarily there to save you. Or perhaps we ought to review?

Applying The Writing Process To Your Resume

1: Make notes. Everything you can think of. Now's the time to think long and hard about your jobs. Make a painfully boring list of all your duties for each one (including that remarkable performance opening doors; you can edit it out later). List all of your clients. All of your accounts. Every special project you did for every job. Every accomplishment, no matter how irrelevant (Gold Star for Attendance: Nursery School). If necessary, even do research on yourself. Go through your own files. You'll be surprised at what you forgot. Once again, this is simply gathering raw material and compiling notes for yourself. Don't criticize or edit, just get it all down. Go through the same process for every part of your resumé. And hold on to your list. At some later time, when you're custom-making a resumé, some minor ability, or hilarious misadventure might be just the feather you need.

2: Organize. analyze. develop what you got. In this case, you know what you're making of your ingredients, you're making a resumé. You also understand the purpose of a resumé. So with all that in mind, organize your thoughts into resumé categories. Then use your talents to summarize and generalize; to assert and then demonstrate. Select which details demonstrate your assertions or *implicit* assertions (I am wonderful; I am great). Which seem relevant? Which seem useful? What point does each make? Have you made the point before? Do you need to make it again? Do you need to make it *here*? Ask yourself of every detail you want to include: Is this really important to a would-be employer? And what is this adding— pertinence or clutter?

3: Choose your structure. Which format, at least tentatively, seems to work best? Which categories do you think you have something to say in?

4. Do a draft. You're right. It's awful. Too wordy. Too long. Looks impenetrable on the page. Take heart. You're not finished.

5: Edit. Ruthlessly. Repeatedly. You know what your goal is: to get it down to a page. Remember that every single word has to "tell. Toss out the adjectives. Murder the canned phrases. (Please don't tell me you "maximized sales." If you must, say you boosted, increased, or even "upped" them— a savings of four letters, and a victory for human language in its battle against sludge.) Eliminate pronouns and even, wherever possible, eliminate verbs.

Now examine it for punch. And rhythm. And tone. Yes, tone. Even the ultimate neutrality of a resumé communicates a voice. Have you offered a dead word where you could have used a live one? A bramble-filled phrase where you could have smoothed it out? If so, rewrite it. Again and again.

6: Play with layout. Print shops and copy shops are chock full of examples. And they're all over the net. Google "resumé, format" or "resumé, layout." Or play around on your own. There are only a few rules. Margins should ideally be an inch on all sides. (And yes, you can hyphenate to make the most of your margins.) The font should be forthright and very easy to read, and never smaller than 10 point, though your name and your contact information should be larger— 14 is ideal. After that, use your layout to emphasize your strengths and mumble your weaknesses. Don't crowd your copy. Skip lines whenever you can, and use bullets where appropriate. When everything's mushed together, nothing pops out.

7: Proofread. Again and again. Leave it overnight. And proofread again. Double-check your spellings. Double-check your facts. If there's time, have a friend look it over for good measure.

The following layouts are merely meant to illustrate what can fit on a page (even more can fit if you sweat it) and still be kind to the eye. If you must use a second page— if there's no way around it— consider listing the knock-em-dead highlights on page one, and then tacking on (to each of the entries you want to extend) "details, next page."

KERRY McDONALD

787 West 12th Street, New York City, 10011 (212) 555-1212, kerry@kerry.com

---

SENIOR ART DIRECTOR
Advertising (all media), product concepts, package design

EXPERIENCE:

20xx--present: **Craven & Feral, London, England**
Television, print, outdoor advertising. Major campaigns for 16 accounts, from food to pharmaceuticals, including
: British Motor Works
: Turnbull & Asser
: Mary Quaint Cosmetics
Created concept of "Face Art" make-up for Mary Quaint. Created its products, designed its packaging, designed and executed ads for all media. Designed its web site.

20xx--20xx: **The Sweatshop, Inc., New York, New York**
Art director, television, print. National campaigns for
: Nabisco (20 products)
: Ronzoni pastas and sauces
: Aunt Maudie's Tea
Redesigned CozyTime package for Aunt Maudie and repositioned the product, contributing to +23% sales

19xx-20xx **Esquire Magazine**, Art Director

AWARDS: Golden Pen, London Art Directors Guild, 20xx and 20xx
For BMW "Drive," and Cadbury's "Chew"
Andy, New York Art Directors Club, 20xx, 20xx, 20xx
For Nabisco: "Ritzy," "Gooey,." Aunt Maudie: "Cheers"

EXHIBITS: Taste Gallery, London, 20xx
3 oils in a show called "Contemporary Genius"

PUBLICATIONS: "What It's Like to be Called a Contemporary Genius," London Times, March 22, 20xx

PROJECTS: Posters for "Save Darfur," Citizens for Justice, 20xx

MEMBER: London Art Directors Guild
New York Art Directors Club

EDUCATION: Ivy College, BFA, 19xx

KERRY McDONALD

787 West 12th Street,, New York City, 10011 (212) 555-1212, kerry@kerry.com

---

Objective: Assistant buyer, women's sportswear

Experience:

The Slot, New York City, 20xx- present

Branch Manager

: Contribute ideas for increasing sales and broadening inventory at monthly meetings with company management.

** One such idea (co-ed dressing rooms) was linked to a 30% increase in sales.

** Another, for including a line of topless t-shirts, was instantly successful, covered as a New York Magazine "Best Bet," and continues to sell $500,000/year.

: Select lead items for 2 street windows and in-store displays

: Responsible for weekly inventory control

: Plus training and supervising staff of 14

Galingblooms, New York City, 20xx-20xx

Sales; Women's Sportswear

ADDITIONAL SKILLS:

Fashion Photography
Windows "Inventory Managment" program.

PROJECTS:

Contributed to fashion photography exhibits:
The Darkroom (Gallery), New York City
The Pettifog Gallery, Burlington, VT

CONTINUING EDUCATION:

Fashion Institute of Technology, New York City (to present)

"Marketing the Future."
"Trends in Sportswear" "
"Designing for Women"
"Inventory Management"
"Buying the Bridge Collection"

PRIMARY EDUCATION:

Hunter College, BA, 20xx

10.
PITCHES, PROPOSALS AND PRESENTATIONS
(AND HOW TO PROTECT WHAT YOU'VE PITCHED AND PROPOSED)

Beyond getting assigned to create the Magna Carta or a page of *The Great Gatsby,* the most hard-to-accomplish writing jobs that mankind has had to face entail selling a new idea. Or, to put that another way: pitches, proposals and presentations.

Alas, this particular category of writing is so broad and heterogenous, so beholden to local whim, that it defies any impositions. When groping about for a formula, the smartest thing you can do is to glom a successful sample. (If you're trying to pitch a book, get the pitch of a book that sold. If you're writing a presentation for your own or another company, get a look at a presentation that your own or the other liked.) Analyze its arguments, analyze its format, analyze its style. If you can't get a winning sample, you're alone with The Seven Steps and the art of strategic thinking.

Let's begin with strategic thinking. Your goal is to (literally or figuratively) sell your stuff. So perhaps, before you launch into doodling about the details, you'd be notably better off to wrack your brain for a rationale (which is something like a rationalization, only saner). Or to offer a finer line:

A RATIONALE IS A LIST OF REASONS
THAT OSTENSIBLY PREMISE AN ACTION.

The action you want is his (you want him to buy your stuff— which could mean your ideas, your service, your project, your plan, or yourself). The rationale is the part where you offer him the sensible reasons he ought to do it.

Keeping, as always, your specific reader in mind (or his company, foundation, superiors or board), what is the rationale that you think might convince him?

What follows are but a few of the usual kind of thoughts.

Your [idea], you want to convince him:

: Solves a problem he knows he has.

: Solves a problem that, remarkably, he *doesn't* know that he has but which you're now of a mind to tell him.

: Fits in with his known goals.

: Expands on his known goals.

: Appeals to a known market.

: Creates an additional market.

: Is exciting, daring and new— so it's certain to make him money.

: Is exactly like something else— which *already* has made him money. (Either him, or his competition.)

Not all— or perhaps any— of these angles may apply to whatever it is you're doing, but whatever you want to prove to him, the operative word is "prove." You can't simply tell him, you actually have to show him. Perhaps with statistics, perhaps with a pie chart, perhaps with an illustration or maybe with sheer chutzpah— as long as you can (seemingly) appear to back it up.

Let's attempt an experiment. Let's suppose that (for the first time ever in history) you've created Superman— the character and the strip. You've sold it as a comic book (the very first edition is, amazingly, in your hand) and now you want to offer it to secondary markets.

— A popular brand of cereal, to use on its boxes, and perhaps as its iconic television spokesman.

— A textbook publisher, to use in a series of illustrated readers for the second to fourth grades.

Now Superman is Superman. The exact same character, the exact same narrative, the exact same strip. So how would you pitch it to the two other buyers? How can you convince them that it "fits with their known goals" and "appeals to their market"? What kind of statements would you make at the very start? Or to put that another way, what's the rationale?

Since I'm absolutely certain you'll do nothing with this assignment if I instantly spill some beans, I'll divert them into a footnote[1] (which you'll find on the next page) and proceed to another point.

While obviously not every pitch or presentation will require a rationale, the fact is that most will be immeasurably aided if you open with a précis— something that tells your reader, clearly and concisely, what he's about to read and, further, what you want him to *notice* in what he reads.

Don't make him work. Don't make him think. Most people actually hate to have to think— it takes time and gives them a headache— or within a corporation, they're actually scared to think. Then, too, it's human nature to see what you're told to see and to think what you're told to think. For instance, if I say to you, "Don't think of elephants," you probably think of elephants— simply because, by saying it, I've put them into your head. If I show you a painting that's entirely painted white except for one red dot in the lower left corner, and if, before I show it, I talk about the artist's astonishing use of red, you will, if nothing else, focus instantly on the red. You'll look for it immediately and, therefore, see it.

Your design in a précis:

MAKE YOUR READER SEE RED.

In other words, don't just abandon the guy at WheatyFlakes to figure out for himself why he's reading about your hero. Direct him, right from the start. Page One of your presentation.

Even your cover page is carrying information. Aside from your name and your contact information, it should always include a title (*Superman: Embodying Strength Through Nutrition*; *Pet Care Services for Hospital-bound Patients; Custom Software for the Small Business; "Family and Neighbors," Proposal for a half-hour television sit-com*).

THE RATIONALE VS THE MUSE

Advertising agencies, just for example, are big on rationales. Writers and artists universally despise them. Art isn't logical. Nor is it particularly rational either. A strategy, yes, should be logical and rational, but the

1 **About Superman**. As a model of physical fitness, he's the perfect choice for a cereal that's loaded with real nutrition. As a choice for a children's reader, he's an educational tool, a living model of solid values, teaching truth, justice, virtue, public service, and moral might, not to mention the underrated virtue of modesty. He also teaches children not to bully the Clark Kents because, hey, you never know...

execution isn't.

Rationales are supposedly done before-the-fact. Before you board the commericial. Before you think of the ad.

The rationale says: "The reason we believe we should go with something funny is... [fill in the blank.]" "The reason the photographs should only be close-ups..." "The reason the logotype should definitely be green..."

Well, okay, but as you and I know, the reason that the logotype is green is that it's green. That something intuitive told you it was green. The reason the photograph is close is that it's close. You fooled around with printing it and close looked the best. And the reason to recommend a slapstick commercial is that that's the one you wrote (or the best of what you wrote).

Rationales by artists are always—almost always— done *after* the fact. The muses hardly ever dance well within a box. So the best way around it is to let the muses scamper wherever they want to go and then wait till they've landed and build the box around them.

THE PROCESS AND THE PITCH

From the rationale on, your best buddy will be The Process.

Start making notes. You might want to give yourself some categories first— to pre-organize or possibly stimulate your thoughts. What categories fit? (Design? Implementation? Savings? Cost?) How about the News Questions? *What's* your idea? Make plenty of random notes. Attempt to define it briefly, attempt to define it colorfully, attempt to define it clearly. *How* does the thing work? *Who* is required to do it? (Which people will be involved? And who are you to manage it? What are your credentials, your track record, skills?) *When* can it be accomplished? And *Why*— from the buyer's point of view— should he buy it?

Now organize, analyze and develop what you've got. You're supposedly making a case. What specifics will help you make it? Which general cans of peas do you want to open or leave alone? Does your message, as a whole, have an overriding theme that's reflected in all its parts? If you haven't pre-organized, get it together now.

Examine it for a while; keep thinking and making notes, then:

Play around with a structure. What is the best order? What order will build a case? What order will build it clearly in a line of progressive steps? What order will hook your reader?

Just for a stray example:

: This is your problem.

: This is my solution.

: This is the nitty gritty:

a) how it works, b) what it saves, c) what it costs.

: This is why I, or my company, should do it.

No problem? Create one (or invent a solution anyway): How to increase your sales by exploiting a broader market. Why you should modernize your billing procedures. Why installing a trampoline would benefit your bank.

Here's another kind of structure for another kind of pitch:

: A brief (brief!) description of what your company does.

Wombat Incorporated is the largest importer of marsupials in Tennessee. We also provide training in kangaroo husbandry, bandicoot breeding and koala nutrition. For 23 years we have served as advisers to the International Board of Marsupial Preservation and our staff of 18 has won national awards.

: Here's who we are. (Blurbs on your key players.)

: These are the kinds of problems we successfully solve.

: Here's how we solve them in a truly unique way.

: Here's why we solve them a lot better than anyone else.

: Here's a brief list of who we've already solved them for.

If your pitch, of necessity, has to be detailed and relatively long, then consider beginning with **a one-page overview**—a summary that touches on all the important points. This All-At-A-Glance approach will invariably warm the heart of any haven't-got-time executive, and the exercise of writing it will help you to focus in on what's important within your pitch.

Another thing to consider when you're fooling around with structure is the virtue of **an appendix**. Or two, three, or four. An appendix can function like a giant footnote. Instead of interrupting your section about Financials with a flurry of charts and numbers, you can stick them all at the end, while assuaging your reader's jitters with a "Please see Appendix A."

Now it's time for your first draft. This should not be done in a hurry. Rework it a million times. Let it lie around for a week. And then tackle it once again.

Edit, edit, edit. Clarity is your king. Brevity is your goal. Leave nothing to inference. Say what needs to be said. Say it clearly and say it once— meaning say it without redundance. Pare it down to the bone. Keep it human and straightforward. Your running order should build in a clear progression of logic, so ask yourself: Does it? If it doesn't, play with the order. Finally:

Do a layout. Subheads will be a help. So will bullets, boxes and bolding. Where will you place your photos? Where will you place your charts? How large or small should they be? Play around with it. Let it sit. Play some more with it. Then proof.

Finally, you'll want to show it off with a good binder, or folder, or cover. Please don't go overboard with overpriced opulence; it smacks of hyperbole. Do, however, invest in something tasteful, solid and clean.

The PowerPoint Pitch

PowerPoint pitches are so This Minute that they're teetering on the verge of being So Last Year. But This Minute they surely are. And even when you're not in a room in front of an audience, you may still have to deliver such a pitch on a CD since the current crop of executives would rather engage a disk than a tangible stack of paper. What we're talking about with PowerPoint, or one of its newer rivals, is a simple series of slides. These slides, which accompany a verbal or written pitch, will supposedly call attention to... your most powerful points. Very often, they're pretty silly. When you mention, in your audio track, "...our three major goals," the slide, like a graphic chorus, echoes

Three Major Goals:

Satisfying customers.

Satisfying shareholders.

Satisfying needs.

One hopes, if you're writing this particular kind of pitch, that you'll try to be a lot more imaginative with your prose and more telling with your points than the dreariness up above.

The Three Best Reasons Not To Do It Yourself:

1) You'll get angry.

2) You'll mess up.

3) In the end, you'll have to hire us anyway.

Then, too, if you have to do a slide presentation, your skills as an editor are the ones you'll want to use. Limit your slide count to 10 slides max, and limit their content to 3 or, at the very most, 4 bullets each. This again is an exercise in knowing what's important and in cutting right to the chase. Obviously, visuals are much more informative when they're showing something— how can I put this— visual. The floor plan of the building. The beautifully iced wedding cake. The 17 Emmys. The charm of a small koala.

The particular vacuity and banality of The Slides is hilariously illustrated by Peter Norvig as he PowerPoints Lincoln's Gettysburg address, designed with, as he puts it, a "completely gratuitous graph" of those "87 years." Please do take a look. http://norvig.com/Gettysburg

Okay. With that said, there will certainly be occasions when a pie chart is important, as indeed there may be occasions when a point should be spelled out. But if your own isn't one of them— and you still have to send a disk— consider making a slick little couple-of-minutes film. And what I mean is: Instead.

Protecting Your Ideas

You've invented the better mousetrap, you've created the perfect plot, you've come up with a new system for smashing atoms or training fleas. Further, you haven't done it in your role as salaried serf; you've accomplished it on your own. (Caution: what you do on your company's time and space and what you do as a paid employee is the property of your boss. Which doesn't mean that a rival won't attempt to say it was his and reap the Brownie points and the raise.)

The rule, in a nugget here, is *Caveat vendor* (or, to state it less artfully, *Seller, beware*).

**THE BETTER YOUR IDEA IS,
THE MORE IT'S APT TO GET STOLEN.**

This is simply a fact of life. Like the sharks eating the minnows or the bees screwing the flowers. Stealing a hot idea remains a civilly suable crime— one that's easy enough to accomplish and disconcertingly hard to prove. And in line with American justice, every thief is an innocent lamb until the second you prove him guilty. And in order to prove him guilty— here's the huge, improbable catch— you will have to amass your evidence *in advance of* the actual crime.

Metaphorically, at least, your idea is your baby. If you want to prove to a court that your baby was kidnapped, you'll initially have to prove that there *was,* in fact, a baby, and then that the kid was yours. And the first way to do that is to get it a birth certificate. Name, parent's name, brief description and date of birth.

And, no, we're not talking about a copyright here because—

IDEAS CAN'T BE COPYRIGHTED...

Neither, by the way, can a title or a name.[2]

BUT THEIR BIRTHS CAN BE REGISTERED.

How? When your brainchild first enters your brain, and before you've blatted to anybody, write the thing down.

Begin with its essence. ("Idea for a comic strip possibly titled *Superman*. Hero's this apparently nerdy kind of a guy except he comes from another planet, has supernatural powers, and works them to fight crime.") Now go back to the nitty-gritty— every tittle that's in your

2 For a list of what you can copyright, see www.copyright.gov or legalzoom.com

head. (Krypton, Daily Planet, x-ray vision and Lois Lane.) Add a sketch of your caped hero. Sign your name and the day's date. Make a photocopy of everything. And now take the original, ink-signed copy and mail it, by Registered Mail, to yourself. Do not seal the envelope with anything but a lick (using tape will make it invalid). Pleasantly ask the clerk to put the date stamp on the back, on the seam of the sealed flap.

That's it. Once delivered, never open it unto death. Write "Superman" on the front so you'll forever know what it is, and then file it away safely.

Your officially dated document, as long as it isn't opened or otherwise tampered with, serves as your registration and will—at least arguably (but, note: not definitely)— back you up in a court.

If you want to go even further, there are several ways to go. If you've got an agent or lawyer, send a copy to him or her with a dated covering letter. If you also belong to a guild or any other professional group, call and ask about registration. Many groups will provide the service either free or at little cost. Keep a copy of all your letters; make a copy of all receipts.

Once you've used any of these methods of registration, make a note on the title page of any subsequent presentation. *Registered: [Name of professional organization]* or otherwise *Registered: [September, 2010.]* This can function like a giant *Beware of Dog* in your front window. It doesn't make you burglar-proof, but frightens a lot of thieves.[3]

And remember, button your lip.

YOUR FIRST AND BEST LINE OF DEFENSE IS YOUR OWN TEETH.

Don't blabber and don't brag. The best way to keep a hot diamond mine to yourself is to keep it to yourself.

Your second line of defense is The Collier Brothers defense. And for those too young to remember, the two brothers were lonely loons whose psychotic hobby was saving paper. Save every scrap of your notes. All your sketches, even the duds. Every noodle, doodle and draft. And write the date of the day you doodled.

3 This doesn't, of course, apply to any stuff you do for your office. But mailing yourself a copy is appropriate just the same.

TAKING BABY OUT FOR A WALK

For many kinds of proposals, a good agent or rep can help, but even agents can rip you off. Don't throw darts at the Yellow Pages. Pick your agent with loving care. Even then, when you've shown your baby, write a letter that says you did.

Dear Agent X: I'm so happy you liked my Superman and agreed to represent it. Would you like some additional copies?

Dear Agent X: Thanks for taking the time to review my ideas for Superman. I'm sorry you didn't like it, but perhaps we can get together on another set of ideas.

What you're doing here is simply creating a legal record— written proof that you showed your baby to Agent X on the X of June.

Why do you need a record? If your agent suddenly quits, or develops a case of amnesia, or a roaring conflict of interest, there's your written and dated proof. (Keep a copy of all your letters.)

Now suppose you haven't an agent but you manage, all on your own, to get a meeting with Steele & Snipe. Here's the advice of a wary lawyer. Please apply it to any pitch or proposal you're apt to make:

"Before you talk about your idea, tell your potential buyer that if he uses your idea, in any way at all, you're expecting to get paid— at a fee you can mutually agree upon later. Don't take this obvious premise for granted. Wait till he answers. Then, if he does, hand him a copy of your written presentation and then, and only then, start to make your verbal pitch.

"After the meeting, send a follow-up letter, confirming the meeting, repeating the ideas presented in the meeting as well as his agreement (if only a nod of the head) to pay you if it's used. This follow-up letter constitutes a contract in the eyes of the law, and any infringement is a cause for action based on Breach of Contract."- *Gilbert Lasky, speaking to the Writers Guild of America in the late 1980's.*

Let me add my own notes.

While the purpose of the letter is to arm yourself neatly with some legal ammunition, you'd be better off to disguise it as a sweet simple exercise in civilized manners.

Dear Mr. Snipe: It was so nice meeting you on Friday afternoon and I'm thrilled with your interest in my flea-training kit, and especially in my methods of inducing electric shock. Though we only made a general agreement about a payment, I'm sure we can come to a specific arrangement that will satisfy us both if you decide to go further.

Or:

Dear Mr. Snipe: I wanted to thank you for the meeting on Monday night, though I'm sorry my idea for Flea-o-matic didn't click. If, perhaps in retrospect, all or even parts of Flea-0-matic gains in appeal, I assume that you'll honor our financial agreement.

Mr. Snipe and his partner will think twice about ripping you off.

Now, roll it back. If, when you're meeting him, he *doesn't* agree to pay, or starts hedging or making noises about terms you wouldn't accept, say no, or, more tactfully, respond that you'll think it over, smile nicely and run for the hills. Give him nothing; tell him nothing.

If he asks you to sign a waiver as a pre-condition for meeting, *don't* sign the waiver, don't smile, and run for your life.

If he asks you to make some changes— without payment and without any formal written agreement— don't agree, but be open-minded— or appear to be open-minded. "Um, gee, I don't know. But let me hear what you'd like to see." Make notes on the guy's ideas. If he's planning to rip you off, chances are that he'll rip you off along the lines that he's now presenting. And no matter how atrocious you believe his ideas to be, look thoughtful but don't argue. (Argue later should you decide to go along with him part way.) When he's finished, smile sweetly again and tell him you'll think it over. Commit yourself to nothing. Go home and give it some thought. But whatever it is you're thinking, type your notes, carefully date them, and then squirrel away your copy (or register-mail a copy— one to yourself and one to your agent, representative or lawyer).

The question arises: Is this palpable paranoia?

The answer is: Yes. But better paranoid than conned.

11.
LETTERS OF AGREEMENT AND OTHER KINDS OF CONTRACTS

At some time or another in the course of your career, you may be asked to sign a short-term or even a long-term contract. Contracts are very, very serious business. They're legally binding. Which means they can tie up your money, your freedom, your work, or your life. And unless or until you're very certain of what you're doing, when it comes to either signing or creating a contract, the watchword to watch is:

DON'T TRY THIS AT HOME.

It's well worth the money to invest in a lawyer or a similar kind of expert. And again, if you belong to a professional organization, it may kindly offer legal information at no cost. But any way you do it, hiring a lawyer, even once in your life, can be a wonderful investment. You can study what he did—which lines he deleted, which words he inserted—and the next time— maybe— you can handle it on your own.

In general, a contract is a legally binding statement about the rights and the obligations of everybody involved. There are several kinds of contracts: the verbal agreement, the letter of intent, the letter of agreement, and the darkly official bear-traps that the lawyers lay for the lambs.

Let's begin from the bottom up.

THE LAWYERLY CONTRACT

You've seen them in other contexts. They're deceptively preprinted to appear as though graven in stone. They are *never* graven in stone. The most helpful and intelligent information I can give you is the single, insightful, indubitable fact:

THERE IS NO SUCH THING AS A "STANDARD CONTRACT."

Commit that to memory.

Whenever somebody offers you a formally printed contract full of truly disgusting clauses, their position, when you object, will be to say, "It's our standard contract." The implication, of course, being that everybody who's worked for them has signed that particular contract, that it's that contract or nothing.

They are lying through false teeth.

The (quote) "standard contract" is the boilerplate bear-trap that's offered to the desperate, the stupid or the young.

It's the first price quoted in a Persian market. It's your opening to bargain; that's all it ever is. They'll insist that it's otherwise and try to sound tough. Because the thing they call "standard" gives everything to them and hardly anything to you.

Do not sign a contract when it's wiggled under your nose. Take it home, read it over, call a lawyer (or a cop).

Do not sign a contract till you understand the breadth of its baroque ramifications which are usually not apparent to the innocent or the kind. Remember: all contracts are written in Legalese which has little to do with English. In fact, to put it to bed:

**LAWYERLY ENGLISH IS TO REGULAR ENGLISH
WHAT SUDOKO IS TO KINDERGARTEN TIC-TAC-TOE.**

And here's another thing you can ponder.

**WHILE A CONTRACT CAN (AND DOES)
MEAN MORE THAN IT OPENLY SAYS,
IT MEANS WHAT IT OPENLY SAYS.**

I was once given a contract with a truly terrible clause (that I'd work for nobody else until the publisher published the book that I was being contracted to write) but was told by The Man Himself, "Aw c'mon, we'd never enforce it." I nodded and told him, "Swell. Then why don't I add a clause that I'm entitled to break your head if you decline to publish the book. Because… c'mon, I'd never enforce it."

No matter what anyone says, it's what the *contract* says that's the point. Take nobody's verbal assurance. Accept nobody's explanations or their efforts to soft-pedal ("Oh that! What it *really* means is just…"). Just forget it. Don't sign it. Not on your life. If that's what it really means, ask them sweetly to put it in writing.

A few other tips below, in the sections involving Letters, may be helpful in different ways, but the general rule is this:

Never sign a contract that will make you moan in your sleep. And secondly, if you do, at least be conscious of what you've done. That you've soberly and intentionally made a compact with the devil and, for Much Higher Purposes, allowed yourself to be had.

THE LETTER OF AGREEMENT

A letter of agreement looks like a normal letter (from *Dear* to *Sincerely*) but don't let it fool you. After you've signed it, it's as legally binding as a formal contract. It *is* a contract; it spells out your mutual rights and obligations.

If you freelance for a company, especially a small one, they're likely to send you a letter of agreement. In which case you'll usually have to amend it before you sign your name (because usually, no matter how Dear and Sincere, it will probably hold a trap).

NEVER SIGN A LETTER YOU HAVEN'T READ CAREFULLY AND CONSIDERED CAREFULLY— INCLUDING ITS IMPLICATIONS.

Legal documents are *about* implications. Their fuzzy generalizations will legally apply to all conceivable situations, no matter how fiendish and no matter how remote.

Does the letter say you'll "attend all necessary meetings"? You could find yourself attending 170 meetings, a thousand miles from home. And all of them based on— and only based on— the other guy's perverted definition of necessity. You might want to amend that. You might want to say that for the project in question and the money in question you'll "attend [3] meetings at a mutually agreeable location and time." ("Mutually," please note, is a legally magic word.) You might want to add that beyond [3] meetings, their cost will be an additional [$x] an hour.

Apply this analysis to every clause on the page. Ask yourself, fiendishly, "What could this entail?" and then modify it accordingly.

Modifying a contract is as easy as using a pen— cross *out* what you want deleted, caret *in* what you want to add, and then initial the change in the margin. (This means, add your initials, and you have to add them in pen.)

Here's another trap in the sand.

While the contract or letter will invariably specify *what* you'll be paid, you might also want to nail down *when* you'll be paid and exactly what happens if they hate what you've done. Let's explore that in detail.

The Money Part Of The Deal

For a freelance project, are you getting an advance? If you aren't, you should. An advance is meant to pay you, up front, for your time. Depending on the project, it's usually from a third to a half of the final fee. If your contract or letter specifies an advance, insert the word "nonrefundable" before it. Or to put that succinctly:

NEVER TAKE AN ADVANCE YOU COULD HAVE TO GIVE BACK.

An advance is meant to pay you— not for your work— but for the time you spend working. So your iron rule should be that since you can't get your time back, they can't get their money back.[1] Besides, chances are that you've already spent the money on the fundamentals of living. So how would you pay them back?

Are you getting a down payment or deposit against a purchase? Consider the costs to yourself. Are your own expenses involved? Are you losing an alternate sale? Is the [object] losing its value? Decide what you want to say. Is is totally nonrefundable? Partially nonrefundable? Refundable up to [a date]? Whatever it is you settle upon, be certain to get it in writing.

NEVER SIGN ANYTHING THAT SAYS IF THEY DON'T LIKE IT THEY DON'T HAVE TO PAY YOU A DIME.

This is known as working "on spec." And while there may be a situation in which the prize at the other end is so tantalizing and wondrous that you're willing to take a chance, never do it for bread and butter. Your

1 You may, in a fair contract, be obliged to return the money in the case of your "nonperformance." Meaning that you didn't give them any time at all, or any work at all, or you totally blew their deadline. But otherwise, never sign a pledge that you'll give it back..

contract ought to specify a "kill fee" or "buyout" or implicitly include it in a logically-timed series of nonrefundable installments.·

Otherwise, you're in trouble. Too many things can happen— having nothing to do with your work— that will give them the grounds to stiff you. Like: the guy who hired you quits (or even worse, the fellow was fired). Or they suddenly change the ground rules, or discontinue the line, or lose the budget or lose the account. None of this would give them any legal grounds for defaulting; however, if you've agreed that mere "dislike" is sufficient grounds, they'll simply tell you they "didn't like" it.

Which leads us to something else.

The When Part Of The Payment

When do you want the advance, and when do you want the balance?

Once again, you should spell it out. If you won't begin the assignment till the day you get the advance, better put that into the contract. (For assignments that come with a deadline, this will give them reason to pay.) If their original contract or letter says they'll cut you the final check "upon acceptance" or "on approval," what they're saying is "if we like it" and in terms of the crucial *when*, it's "when we *share* with you that we like it." In other words, they can sit on the thing for 60 or 90 days before they even give it a glance, then decide that they want revisions, then decide that they want some more, and then withhold their vaunted "approval" till... however long they can stall.

So how can you fix the contract to get your money before you're dead? If it specifies the final part of the payment is "on acceptance," then consider amending it thus: "Within [20] days of acceptance which either has to be given, or otherwise denied, within [7] days of delivery."

Indeed, you may still have to deal with a bunch of revisions, but at least you've speeded it up. Further, you can specify how many revisions are included within your price. And finally, you can fix it so your payment's in three parts: advance, on delivery, and "upon final acceptance," which at least covers the time spent revising the cursèd thing.

Writing (As Opposed To Just Signing) An Agreement

If you don't get either a contract or a letter, depending on the circumstance, you might want to send one. For instance, if you're hired to decorate a restaurant or photograph a wedding (or do, in fact, anything for an individual client or a very small business).

Then, too, you'll want to have one if you're hiring somebody else.

Or you're engaged in collaboration.[2]

In either case, you might send a letter of agreement or a letter of intent (for which, see below).

The rather major difference between a letter of agreement and a letter of intent is that letters of agreement must invariably be signed at the bottom by both parties.

If you're writing such a letter, type an ending with open blanks—

Signed (Your name) ______________________ date__________

Signed (Their name)______________________ date__________

—and leave your own signature blank.

Send two hard copies. Instruct your recipient to sign and return both, and then, when you get them, sign and return one (so that each of you possesses one double-signed copy).

As to what you say in the letter, pay attention to what you write. A legal generalization is a double-edged sword. A loophole can hang you. On the other hand, you can nail things down to such an extent that you've hammered yourself to the wall. Again, if it's possible, get thee to an attorney.

THE LETTER OF INTENT

The letter of intent is a one-way letter (it needn't be mutually signed) in which one of the two parties states his own binding intentions and his opposite's (similarly binding) obligations. This is usually, but still not exclusively, applicable if the terms in the letter have been previously discussed. It says, for example: *Dear Harry: This is just to confirm what we discussed...* and then lists what you discussed. Harry, of course, can always

2 If two or more people engage in collaboration, their agreement should specify their "separation of rights" among many things it should specify. Again, see a lawyer (or be ready to see red).

deny that you discussed it, or deny that he got the letter, which is why Registered Mail, Return Receipt was invented.

The letter of intent leaves the ball in your partner's court. If he doesn't respond by arguing or doesn't respond at all, you're entitled to think it's tacit and to premise your acts thereon, though you might want to spell it out: *If I don't hear from you otherwise by Monday, the 23rd, I'll assume this meets your approval.*

A letter of intent can also introduce him to your terms for the first time, though in that case it's best to have his letter of acceptance, or his countersignature or, otherwise, his check.

Let's take the example of a letter (of either agreement or intent) for photographing a wedding.

Dear Mr. Capulet: This letter will confirm the terms of our agreement. My total fee for the job will be [$3000] which includes up to [50 5x7] prints of your choice. Our schedule will be this: After I've received a [$500] nonrefundable advance, I'll be photographing Fido and Juliet's wedding from 2 PM to 7 PM, July 21st, at both the Santa Lucia Church on Riverdale Avenue and your home in New Rochelle. I'll be taking approximately [200] shots, and will show you the contacts by [July 31], at which time I'll collect an additional nonrefundable [$1000] deposit. The [$1500] balance will be due on delivery of the prints you've selected, about [20] days later. The negatives will then become your sole and exclusive property. This letter will serve as our full agreement. Your check for the advance will signify your acceptance of all the foregoing terms.

This letter will protect you from many potential griefs. That Mr. C (who will be a little drunk by 7 o'clock) will expect you to stay till midnight, or to follow the blushing bridelet to the airport in teeming rain to catch her waving her last goodbyes, and then expect you to take 100,000 pictures and print them all— 11x14— and not pay you till nearly Christmastime or never pay you at all because your photos made him look fat.

THE VERBAL AGREEMENT

A verbal agreement— though, yes, better than nothing— basically isn't worth the paper it's not-written on (though it helps if you have a witness or you're seen to be taking notes and then confirm what was said in a letter). {For more, see the section, page 164, "Taking Baby Out for a Walk.")

And always remember that

NO MATTER WHAT YOU'VE BEEN TOLD,
WHAT'LL BITE YOU IS WHAT YOU'VE SIGNED.

12.
INVOICES

Here comes a chapter that (huzzah!) you can skip if you don't sell your labor on a freelance basis, or you never sell the tangible products thereof.

An invoice is the $6 word for the common "bill." And unless you're represented by an agent or other middleman, it's always useful to send one. (Would you ever pay your phone bill if they didn't send you the bill?) Further, you should send one whenever you're sending Stuff, and include it— as a combination invoice and Packing List— right in the very carton. (More on this in a moment.)

If you're working free lance for a major corporation or another Big Business, there are facts you'll need to address:

Has the job been given a number? If so, you'll need the Job Number or Purchase Order number since your bill will have to include it.

Who should you send it to? The Billing, Accounting or Purchasing Department? Or do you need to send it first to the department or specific executive who hired you?

Finally, does the company have special, and totally unguessable, requirements? Do they only accept a bill if it's submitted in triplicate? Or a bill in which the second of three copies is done in pink and the third is canary yellow? Such things have been known to happen and, as savagely dumb as they are, delay your payment by many moons.

Let's digress into something obvious:

A BILL IS ABOUT MONEY.
PAYING MONEY IS NEVER FUN.

Your payer's avowed goal is to keep his money as long as he can. And on top of that, the Automatic Pilots manning Accounting aren't programmed to deal with doubt. Any *i* that hasn't been dotted, any *t* that hasn't been crossed will send them instantly into a tailspin whose solution will be *Default*.

Then, too, there's another facet:

A Bill Is About Money. And Where There's Money, There's Uncle Sam (And Uncle City And Uncle State)

All of them want your money, and all of them are absolutely eager to trip you up on the weensiest little detail. And adding it all together with your payer's entrenched reluctance and his pilots' robotic bents, you can easily trip the trap.

Here's a list of some common trips:

A failure to specify or clarify your status. Your status is either as a salaried "employee" or an "independent contractor," the latter being anyone who isn't "on salary" in the usual sense of the term (the usual sense meaning your employer withholds taxes from whatever it is you've billed). Independent income is initially tax-free (you'll get the full amount that you've billed, minus nothing for kith and kin), though you're expected to pony up, on your own, at the end of the year or end of the quarter (ask an accountant). However, even independent income will be reported and revealed to the IRS in the form of a 1099. Why? Because the government demands to know what you've earned and, not at all incidentally, whoever's paying the bill wants to deduct whatever he's paying as the cost of his doing business.

The above has been a long and very tedious explanation of why— though you bask in the illusion of independence— you may still have to identify your social security number or Taxpayer ID but why, in the next breath, you need to prattle about your Status. (The first, so your employer can rat you out to the feds and thus declare you as a deduction, and the second so he doesn't take the taxes from what you're paid.) If you don't give him the number, he will rarely call to remind you; he will simply sit on the bill.

Note: A small business or a private individual (or anyone being billed for less than $600 a year) likely *won't* require your number so better skip it unless they ask

A failure to separate your fees from your expenses. If you bill them in one bundle and they're issued as one check, it's the total that gets reported. No actual harm's done since you yourself can take the deductions, but accounting for every cab can be an accounting pain in the neck and your old Uncle can get confused. Better, if possible, to keep the transaction clean, sending one bill for expenses and another bill for your work. And, in any case, always keep a copy of all receipts, since even those expenses that you can't bill to your client can be wrangled from Uncle Sam as your legitimate deductions.

A failure to state your terms. "Terms," in this instance, means the terms or conditions that apply to the job or sale. These include, most notably, the date you expect to be paid. If you haven't established a deadline when you're doing your pre-nups, the savvy payer will set it for you. Bottom line will be 90 days. Want it sooner? The better move would be to set it up in advance but, in any case, your invoice ought to end with your stated Terms. Like: *Terms: [30] days.* Then, too, if what you're selling is a three-dimensional Thing, be very clear about terms of sale. (Are the items at stake returnable? Till when? Under what conditions? Every invoice should spell it out.)

A failure to charge taxes in a case where taxes apply, or the equal-but-opposite error of appending them where they don't. As applied to actual labor, and as well to tangible goods, rules will vary from state to state (and even vary from case to case.)[1] Check it out with a local expert. In general, though, you needn't add a tax when you're selling wholesale (i.e., when you sell to a store) nor to individual clients if they live in a different state. Be aware that's a generalization. Check carefully; never guess. Further, if you're actually running a Small Business, you'll invariably need a license, especially if you're "vending," simply meaning you're selling goods. Your licensor (the state) will instruct you in all the rules.

A wholesaler's invoice— a bill you send to a store— should include,

1 In New York, just for example, painting a room for the first time is a nontaxable service; repainting the same room, even seventy years later, is a taxable "repair." Further, buying merchanidise that's part of a final product which itself will be put on sale becomes a purchase without a tax, while the very same merchandise bought for another purpose has a city and state bite. In other words, don't try to dope this out for yourself.

for your own protection, their retailer's (business or resale) number. Usually, too, it includes the "suggested retail" (also known as the "list") price, and the wholesale discount you've agreed to offer. Examples appear below.

Beyond actual billing, if you're shipping a box of goods, you should

ALWAYS INCLUDE A PACKING LIST.

A packing list is obviously a list of the stuff you've packed (in the crate, carton or envelope) along with its specs and cost. Including a packing list— and always keeping a copy— is a excellent form of insurance against a vendor's garden of grief. A packing list can also do a double turn as an invoice, or a double turn as receipt.

What follows are a couple of suggestions about formats (there are actually no rules). Furthermore, the content will vary from case to case and with the needs of your various payers. When in doubt, you can always ask them.

BRIGHT IDEAS

225 WAYWARD LANE **PEARL, UTAH 74623**

INVOICE

BILLING DATE: March 12, 2009

TO: Gyre & Gimbel, Inc.
5760 Madison Avenue
Salt Lake City, UT 74689
Attn: Billing Department

FROM: Karen Bright
SSN: 555-55-5555, Independent Contractor

FOR: JOB #: 6750
Writing/producing 3 radio commericals- "Frobes Instant Water"

FEE...$2000
ADVANCE PAID, 1/31/09..- 1000

AMOUNT DUE: $1000

TERMS (PER CONTRACT): 30 days

BRIGHT IDEAS

225 WAYWARD LANE **PEARL, UTAH 74623**

REIMBURSABLE EXPENSES RE; JOB # 6750

PLEASE ISSUE AS A SEPARATE CHECK

BILLING DATE: March 12, 2009

Recording. Alpha Studios 1.5 hours @ $100/hr...................$150

Editing/Mixing. Alpha Studios, 1 hr @ 150/hr........................ 150

Talent (Mandy Anson) to bill directly through Gem Agency ------

TOTAL AMOUNT DUE...........$300

TERMS: On receipt

Packing list/ Invoice from:

THE POT SPOT

Handmade pottery. Wholesale/retail
9579 Cantaloupe Vista, Righteous, CA 67981, (301) 555-5555

To: The Bumble Shop
5760 N. Hamilton Road
Carmine, CT 55555

Billing date: March 1, 2009

Re: Your PO: 76549

Invoice #: 9-6577

Resale #: xxxxx, CT

Order Received: 2/17/09 Shipped: 2/22/09 Via: FedEx Ground

Tracking #:xxxxxxxxxxxxxxxxx

QTY	ITEM #	DESCRIPTION	LIST PER UNIT	DISCOUNT	NET
1	A500	Tureen (azure)	200	-50%	100.00
12	Q750	Soup Bowl (azure)	35	-50%	240.00
				SHIPPING	17.23
				TAX	-------
				TOTAL	$357.73

TERMS:
Full payment within 30 days.
Items returnable within 7 days if shipped in original packing
and received undamaged.
Shipping costs plus a 10% stocking charge will be deducted.

Packing list/ Receipt from:

THE POT SPOT

Handmade pottery. Wholesale/retail
9579 Cantaloupe Vista, Righteous, CA 67981, (301) 555-5555

To: Ms Melanie Trinket
9470 Parkside Avenue
New York, New York 10972

Shipping date: March 1, 2009

Invoice #: 9-6578

Order Received: 2/17/09 Shipped: 2/22/09 Via. FedEx Ground

Tracking #:xxxxxxxxxxxxxxxx

QTY	ITEM #	DESCRIPTION	UNIT PRICE		TOTAL
1	A500	Tureen (azure)	200		200..00
12	Q750	Soup Bowl (azure)	35		480.00
				SHIPPING	17.23
				TAX	----
				TOTAL	697.23

PREPAID: VISA #### THANK YOU.

Items returnable within 7 days if shipped in original packing
and received undamaged.
Shipping costs plus a 10% stocking charge will be deducted.

Carolee's Hang-ups

757 East 75th Street, Apt 2, New York City 10075

INVOICE

Billing Date: May 11, 2010

To: Ms. Melanie Trinket
9470 Parkside Avenue
New York City, 10972

From: Carolee Schultz

For: Wallpapering bedroom

Labor: 8 hours @ $50/hr..$400.00

Supplies (glue, primer)* 37.89

Parking*...32.47

DUE ON RECEIPT........................$470.36

* Home Depot receipts and garage receipt attached

13.
EMAILS, MEMOS, AND MISCELLANEA

Since emails are the most common form of communication—and often encompass memos, assignments, instructions, and (almost) everything else, let's start with:

SOME BASIC TIPS ABOUT EMAILS.

Your first job in an email is to make it easy to read and your second job in an email is to make it easy to answer. So with that much in mind:

1. **Be brief.** Pretend you're being charged about $5 a word. Keep your paragraphs brief and paragraph frequently so your points will pop out. If you have three questions, or you're making three points, number them—literally, 1,2,3— putting each in a separate paragraph. Also consider this: A short clean message says "Psst! Read me now." A long dense message says "<groan> Read me later."

2. **Find a subject line that cuts right to the point.** You are not titling a movie or an article or a book. This is not the time for Creative. If your memo's about the hurricane destroying the cafeteria, please don't title it *Gone With The Wind*. Title it *Hurricane Damage to Cafeteria*.

Specificity's the charm. If you're asking if a supplier has a particular thing in stock, don't muddle around with subjects like *Product Inquiry* or even the more informative *Turntable parts,* go directly to: *Garrard Turntable parts for model 71-20.*

Also, if you possibly can, keep it short. Most email inboxes preview the subject in a max of 30 characters and cut off the rest. Design your subject line to front-load the most important part within 30. If your subject is: *Tuesday morning's meeting at Crandleberry postponed till Thursday morning*, the inbox will cut you off somewhere around *Cran* and your reader may well decide, "Ho-hum, I can read it later," and meanwhile give the nod to a conflicting meeting for Thursday. Your better bet, then, would be something along the lines of: *Tues meeting —> Thurs 9 AM.*

Another bit of courtesy: If the whole of your message can be crammed into the subject line, say it in the subject line and add "EOM" which is short for "end of message." This saves your reader the time of opening the message. So, for example: *Tues meeting—> Thurs 9AM EOM*

Suppose you've got several subjects to discuss. The change in the meeting *and* a change in the agenda. How do you title it? One way would be: *2 Changes re Crandleberry*. Another is— simply send two separate messages, each with an easily refindable title: *Tues meeting—> Thurs 9 AM* and *Agenda changes: Thurs meeting.* And note, I said "refindable." Tomorrow. Next week. A month and a half later. Which, your reader wonders, among the billion tags in his inbox, is the memo about the agenda. Ah! There it is. *Agenda Changes...)*

This titling specificity applies—in spades— to a continuing correspondence. When you answer an email whose original subject was *Dinner with client*, your computer will make the subject line *Re: Dinner with client.* But if, in your answer, in addition to confirming your Monday availability, you inquire about the office Superbowl pool and, in turn, get an answer about the Superbowl pool plus a question about the change in the Crandleberry agenda... for heavens sake, please change the subject line to reflect it. Otherwise your answer about the Crandleberry budget will appear under the title *Re:Re:Re:Re: Dinner with client.* And who, in his right mind, could ever guess what the thing's about?

It's also considerate, within your subject line, to let your reader know if any action will be required and if the message is— or actually isn't— priority. Such openings on the subject line as *ASAP, RSVP, FYI,* or even *Q:*[1] offer valuable indications.

3. <u>Be selective about greetings.</u> The greeting line in an email is the cyber equivalent of the "Dear Mr. Johnson" at the start of a hard

1 ASAP=As Soon As Possible, RSVP=Respond, Please, FYI=For Your Information, Q:= Question (3 Q's:=3 questions). Each should then be followed by a terse but exact indication of the subject. E.g, *ASAP: Revise Bond Copy. / 3 Q's: re lunch.*

letter. But an email isn't a letter (except, of course, when it is). If it's a *formal* email— a question to a professor, an opinion to a Senator, an answer to a client, a query about a job— then a *Dear Mr. Johnson* or (depending) a *Dear Joe* would be the usual way to go. As a general rule of thumb, when in doubt, it's better to err on the side of formality (no one will be offended by a *Dear Mr. Johnson*) and to later take your cue from the answer of your respondent. If he answers *Dear Alec*, you can answer *Dear Joe*. Emails to strangers or to folks on your own level may (but only *may*) begin with a mere *Hello* or with a chattily casual *Hi*, or with a nothing whatsoever. And in emails to office mates or everyday correspondents, skip the greeting and get to the point.

4. Don't Mumble And Don't Shout. A message done in all capital letters is a shout and is often seen as deranged. A message with *no* capital letters (say, for instance, at the opening of a sentence) is a far-too-casual mumble. Neither is appropriate for business correspondence.

5. Kill half the abbreviations—and all the emoticons. They're usually not helpful and they're usually too cute. If you must use abbreviations, again, as a rule of thumb, use them only in direct and inverse proportion to the formality of the message and the rank of your recipient. At the start of a correspondence, use only abbreviations that are easily— in fact, universally— understood and that perform the important function of actually cutting clutter. Examples of such shorthand might include *BTW, AFAIK, or IIRC* [2] but when in doubt, spell it out.

Emoticons. Ugh. Before committing any of these visual clichés, ask yourself seriously, Why am I doing this? If it even crosses your mind that your clumsy attempt at sarcasm might miss its mark without a nudge-of-the-elbow ;) [wink], or that your joke won't come through without the timpani roll of a :) [smile], then either eliminate the sarcasm and the joke OR— actually take the trouble to clarify your prose. Finally, in an unofficial survey of thirty friends, the hands-down winners of The Most Annoying Thingamajigs To Find In An Email were the sad-face emoti-

---

2 BTW=by the way; AFAIK=As far as I know; IIRC=If I remember correctly.

con :(to stand for "I'm sorry" or "I'm disappointed, too," and the verbal emoticon, *Heeheeheehee.*

6. **When responding to an email, always be precise about what you're responding *to*.** Years ago, in my youth, there was a series of corny riddles that began by giving an answer and then asking What was the question? (The one that stays in my mind was: *The answer is 9 W; what was the question?* The question was ostensibly: *So, Herr Wagner— Do you spell your name with a V?*) Now imagine getting an email that responds— without any elaboration— *9W*. And trying to wrack your brain for the question you must have asked. Do unto others as you'd have them do unto you. Include the previous message along with your fresh response. If the message you got was long and the part that requires an answer is the merest snip in the middle (the part where the writer asked you if you spelled your name with a V), include only the pertinent part of the writer's previous message. My Mac lets me accomplish that by highlighting the passage before I hit the "reply." If your computer doesn't allow for that, then copy and paste the passage onto your answering message. Similarly, too, if you're answering 3 questions, copy and paste the questions, and answer between the pastes. Finally, you can simply make the question part of your answer:

As to the spelling of Wagner, although, when pronounced in German, it sounds like it starts with V, it's always spelled with an opening W. Or to answer you now in German: Nein. W.

7. **When sending a URL, make it easy and make it hot.** A URL— a Uniform Resource Locator— (pronounced You Are Ell) is an address on the web. If you're including one in an email, most programs will make it "hot" (one click and your reader's there— a kind of "Beam me up, Scotty") but many will only do that if you offer the whole address, which means starting the thing off with its tacit opening letters: *http://* Another problem is length. The longer the URL, the more likely it is to break (with only part of it staying hot, producing errors instead of links). As a general rule of thumb, if it spills onto two lines, you can keep it from breaking up by enclosing the whole address between the pillars of

these < > brackets. If it's really horribly long, you can magically make it shorter while preserving its linkability by running it through the shrink machine and cutting it down to size. The machine, at this writing, has its own easy address: http://tinyurl.com. (Just go there and do what it says.) And, finally, never punctuate the end of a URL (no periods, commas, dashes).

8. About sending attachments. Attachments, alas, are like candy from strangers. They might contain poison or the wriggling head of a bug. Therefore, before you send attachments off to a stranger, you'd be wiser to give him warning ("I'll be sending a pdf") or even better to ask permission ("*May* I send you a pdf?") It's also considered etiquette to ask the reader's permission to send attachments of great length, and also to ask first if he can open a... [whatever format you want to send] or just ask him what he prefers.

9. About signatures. Usually your email program offers a choice among several (premeditated one-click) signatures as well as a choice of none. In business emails, at least of a formal nature, at least in the first round (and in any subsequent round where alternative methods of contact could reasonably be required— like a Where should they send the payment, or a Where should they fax the form) a signature line should list all the clearly relevant data: your name, title, company, and all of the ways to reach you (address, phone, fax, or whatever you want to include). An alternative signature should offer the first three:

Marie M. Curie
V.P. of Internal Affairs
Radiant Glow Inc.

10. About Avoiding Sender's Remorse. It's so easy— especially in anger— to hit Send (or just even in sloppy haste). After which, you remember that you sent to the wrong person (or the *terribly* wrong person), or you didn't answer the question, or you sounded totally nuts. The only way to avoid this is to never— and I really mean never— fill in the *To:* (just leave the thing blank) until you've seriously reflected on the stuff of your hasty message. This is equally true for responses. If a small voice in your noggin is rather frantically clearing its throat and hollering "Stop me before I kill again," *remove* the name from the *To:* before you enter your bloody message and don't replace it until you're absolutely certain you're sober and sane and what you've written is what you meant.

AND ALWAYS REMEMBER THIS:
AN EMAIL IS FOREVER.

Even if you've trashed it. Even if your hard drive is hit by an errant meteor and shattered to shards of glass, that email from last September (or September 2002) exists Somewhere to be retrieved. And the District Attorney can find it.

A SHORT COURSE ON THE MEMO

A memo is short for a *memorandum* and a memo is just that: short and cut the random. Ideally, a memo cuts instantly to the chase and stays quick, focussed and snappy.

Yes, it should sound human, but like a human who's in a hurry. A memo should convey— simply *and only* — what the reader needs to know. It should begin with, instead of just build to, the point. If it makes several points, it should make them in a quick clear summary up front, and elaborate on each of them separately later, and possibly under subheads. Think of it as an outline. Think of it as an email.

In fact, customarily, memos these days are sent in the form emails since few occasions remain when the hard stuff would be required, and if your reader thinks that it is, then he's always welcome to print it.

BUSINESS MEMOS AS E-MAIL

It was almost a natural that the two should become one. The form of an e-mail is, quite handily, the proper form for a memo. Grandpa's hard copy always started the same way:

To:

CC:

From:

Date:

Subject:

(That quaint CC used to stand for a "carbon copy" but you can think of it more acutely as a "cyber copy" while you pity the inky fingers of the gens that preceded X.)

As an emailer, however, you've got a choice with your CCs. Blind or out in the open? (Do you want Charlie to know that you're copying Marianne? If not, and if he subsequently learns about it from Harry, will he think you're a dirty sneak? And finally, do you care?) These are things for you to decide and I wouldn't get in the middle of this messy little imbroglio for all the tea in the world. This is utterly up to you. In some cases, you might decide to *To:* to the major players and *CC:* to the FYI's, but this too is a game of politics, specific to where you are.

The Subject line we've already covered up above so we're now ready to cut to—

The Body Of The Memo.

Yes, okay, there are memos and there are memos, depending on their intention, but no matter what they're about, the four fundaments will apply:

Be clear, be brief, be natural, be exact.

Throckheimer meeting now changed to 3:30. Pls notify staff and rebook the brass band. IM me to confirm by 2 today latest.

Would that all memos were as one-step as that. Unfortunately, most of them will be more complex, and your assignment, once again, will be to organize, simplify, and sharpen them to a point.

Perhaps this is illustrated best by a few examples so...these are a few examples.

You've been asked to gather estimates on the costs of painting the office and you're reporting back to the boss.

There are right ways to do it and wrong ways to do it. And almost invariably the long way is wrong.

WRONG AND LONG

Subject: Painting the office

I was asked to get estimates from various contractors on the costs and other details of painting the 7th floor using color sample swatches provided by Barbara.

I discussed the project with 6 different companies, obtaining their names from a variety of sources ranging from the phone book to getting recommendations from others within the building.

The prices I obtained ranged from $7000 (Martin & Son) to $10,000 (both Paladin, Inc. and Cobbler & Spear, though Cobbler couldn't start to do the job till November). Delano Decor wanted $8500 and Dan Fuzziolo wanted $8750 but neither is available till the end of December, which of course is too late.

All of the companies estimated the job could be done in approximately 10 full days, though two of them were willing to work on weekends. Paladin could work both Saturday and Sunday and thus take only 6 days of actual office time, while H.M. Decor could work only Saturdays and thus take 8 days of working-day time. H.M, however, was highly recommended by Wilson Johns, the manager of Wonks on the 40th floor, who felt they were worth the (estimated) $9000 they were asking.

I'm attaching the business cards of all 6 companies in case you have questions to ask them directly, and will be happy to book whichever one you choose. All of them, however, will need to be booked about 3 weeks in advance.

Okay. Your turn. Applying the process (generalize, summarize, organize, edit) do a short, relevant rewrite. Then you can read on

RIGHT AND TIGHT:

Subject: Painting estimates

I discussed the details with 6 companies. All said the job would take 10 days to do. These 3 were the ones who could start in September as you requested:

¶ Martin & Son. Advantage: Low bid. $7000, but only works weekdays.

¶ Paladin, Inc. Advantage: Least disruption. Will work both Sat. and Sun. on 2 weekends. $10,000.

¶ H.M Decor. Advantage: highly recommended by manager of Wonks. Will work 2 Saturdays, but not Sundays. $9000.

Let me know what you want to do or if you have more questions. All require advance booking of 3 weeks so you might want to time your decision accordingly.

Got it? Your boss doesn't need you to summarize the breadth of the assignment, he *gave* you the darn thing. Nor does he care about the companies who couldn't do the job on the right schedule or how you got their names. The rest of the wrong, long and tedious memo was a mind-bending muddle, mixing prices and schedules in a totally disorganized and brain-wracking way. In the right-and-tight version you were organized and offered only news he could use.

THE SECRET OF THE RIGHT-AND-TIGHT MEMO IS STRUCTURE.

Find yourself a structure. Ask yourself relentlessly, What do I need to say? (or, perhaps more logically, What does he need to hear?) Which factoids are relevant and which ones are trucks? (Does he, you'll pester yourself, really need to know this? *Why* does he need to know this? If you can't come up with an answer, cut the item and travel on.) Once you've got it surgically reduced to the fundamentals, you'll be ready to find a structure. How can you organize the relevant set of facts so they can instantly and usefully make the point they're supposed to make?

Here's another situation that impels you to write a memo.

As a creative group head at CYA Advertising, you've attended a meeting with a trio of top execs (John Dortmunder, Alexander Portnoy and Hester Prynne) from a newly-acquired client, Snagpruf Hose. Once again you've presented the agency's recommendations: that they 1) change the sign-off logo to "Great Legs!" and 2) expand the target to include older women (18-45). Apparently they're still not ready to take the plunge, and while they're "seriously considering" the hike in the demographics, they couldn't resist suggesting a few "top of the head" ideas about redirecting the logo— all of which clearly (in your humble opinion) stink— and the matter has been tactfully postponed till the next meeting. Meanwhile, however, they showed you a new item for which they want a couple of trade and consumer print ads by the dawn of October 10th. It's a stretch lace bodysuit in 5 standard colors plus silver Lurex, to retail for $40-$55.

Your assignment: Write a memo to a) the creative team who'll have to do the ads, and b) upper management, reporting on the general conclusions of the meeting.

And yes, that "your" in "your assignment" means...*your,* so please do try it and please try it now. Remember that the key to a good memo is its relevance— the utility of its details— and the clarity of its structure.

Think of what you're writing from your reader's point of view— in this case, your boss's and the toilers in field. What do they need to know so they can do what they have to do? If you think of a few details that haven't been included in the summary up above but that your readers would find useful, make them up and toss them in.

And one more reminder: A memo— even a memo— comes alive with the Seven Steps.

So— on your mark now. Ready? Set? Go.

Possible solutions (don't peek) are below:

Memo to Creative Team (one way to do it):

Subject: Snagpruf— new item, short deadline

HERE'S WHAT IT IS:
> *All-in-one bodysuit. Pantyhose legs with stretch lace torso*
> *In black, white, taupe, navy, sand ($40) silver Lurex ($55)*
HERE'S WHAT THEY WANT:
> *A 4 page insert for Womens Wear Daily*
> *A spread and 2 single pages for the mags*
HERE'S WHEN THEY WANT IT:
> *October 10, 9:30 AM.*
WHEN WE SHOULD MEET (PRELIMINARY SKETCHES):
> *October 7, 1:30 PM.*
PHOTOS OF PRODUCT ATTACHED AS JPEGS

The secret here was not just concision, but organization. The helpful use of subheads, the additional help of bullets.

Memo to your boss (one way to do it)—electronically or on paper:

Subject: Snagpruf client meeting, 10/4

Present: John Dortmunder, Alexander Portnoy, Hester Prynne (+me)
Topic 1: Our long-range recommendations
Upshot: Decisions postponed till next month
Opinion: The going may be rough, but we'll win.
Topic 2: Assignment for trade/consumer print ads
Introducing new item. Deadline: 10/10
Upshot: Details sent to creative
Opinion: No sweat.

About our recommendations:

Expanding the market to "older" (up to age 45) women being "seriously considered." Hangup from Portnoy: "Will we scare off the young broads by chasing after their mothers?" At which point, Prynne shot him such a withering look that (if he lives) he'll come around.

Changing the logo-line, however, will be a trip. Prynne: "Isn't 'Great Legs' sexist or something?" Portnoy: "We want to keep it upscale and smart.... Our target's the working woman." Dortmunder brainstorm: "How's this for the logo? 'Snagpruf Pantyhose work as hard as you do!'" Portnoy shoots back, "Work and PLAY as hard as you do." They all seem to like it. Which should speak for itself.

Upshot: Charlie, I think we need to talk. Let me know when.

You've captured a two-hour meeting in its essence. You've zeroed in on the tenor by selecting the telling quotes. I've, of course, presumed a casual relationship with your boss, and presumed he or she shares a keen sense of irony. You could also take the same set of facts and observations and recast them more formally. In fact, go ahead.

Here's another situation and another kind of memo:

The mayor has been pushing, and the city council pondering, a series of new laws that will affect local restaurants. You've attended a meeting of The Restaurant Council on how these changes, which are fairly wide-ranging, would affect your boss's business. Your assignment is to summarize an all-day meeting, during which you took about a zillion pages of notes, and reduce them to an instantly informative bulletin. Structure will once again be your best friend.

And note: when your email simply cries to be fairly long, send its substance as an attachment. So your email would go like this:

Subject: RC Meeting, Nov. 11

New regulations proposed by City Council. Facts, ramifications and proposed courses of action. Memo attached.

And here's your attachment, also in memo form:

Subject: Provisions and effects of proposed legislation

Proposals would very radically affect:

¶ the food we serve (recipes and portions)
¶ how we present it (menu requirements)
¶ how we treat customers (our role as enforcers)

Expenses would entail:

¶ retraining current staff
¶ employing a full-time nutritionist/mathemetician
¶ purchasing calculators (127 @ $8 each)
¶ potential cost of fines ($50 per infraction)
¶ potential loss of business (re changes above)

Here are the details:

Recipes: *No dish served in a restaurant after April 15 may contain more than .02 grams of cholesterol or 2.75 mg of salt.*

Portions: *No portion of any single food may contain more than 321 calories, and no combination of items on a plate may exceed a limit of 962. Finally, no individual customer may order a full meal (including appetizer and dessert) whose total calories exceed 1200.*

Menus: *Should prominently warn all diners of the 1200 calorie full-meal limit and the fines to be imposed for exceeding that limit. Further, they should warn that the portions of inherently calorie-laden food will be proportionately smaller, and should estimate the size. (Ice cream portions may, in most cases,* *consist of no more than 2-3 teaspoons, though those who've ordered only shredded carrots for an entree may receive 4 to 6.)*

Tables: *Must provide either pencil and paper or a solar-powered calculator. Tables may not provide sugar or salt. Requests for ketsup must be calculated in to the overall count (on a per-plop basis to be monitored by the waiter).*

Enforcement and Fines: *Wait staff must double-check the customers' calculations, or, if requested, calculate for them. In case of disagreement, the decision of the waiters shall be deemed as final. If the 1200 calorie limit is exceeded, both customer and waiter will be fined $50, with a jail term not to exceed 7 months for persistent (meaning "more than 3 time") offenders.*

Protest Action: *Attend council hearing, November 22, 10:30 AM, Room 3, City Hall. Prepare to testify. For more information and political updates, call Merrill McAndrew @ Restaurant Council.*

Once again, the emergent key to clarity is structure. Once again— as in the note to your advertising boss— you began with an overall look at the bottom line, and then (and only then) started plunging into specifics.

INSTRUCTIONS ABOUT INSTRUCTIONS

So there it was, a no-kidding 97 degrees, my air conditioner died, I was working on a deadline, and my half-year-old printer went suddenly out of ink. At least, I thought hopefully, the printer was no sweat. After all, I had an extra cartridge right in the drawer and the procedure should be a snap. A bucket of sweat later, no snap was forthcoming. The corpse of the dead cartridge was refusing to snap out. I tugged, pulled, yanked, pried, jiggled and broke a nail. I began to consider a butter knife. I began to consider the consequences of considering a butter knife, and looked for a brighter notion. Aha! it finally came to me: The Book of Instructions! I found the book of instructions which, alas, included nothing along the lines of *Replacing Cartridge*. It did, however, offer a small hint on *Inserting Cartridge* whose full and complete instructions read in total:

—> Insert cartridge.

True, this suggestion went along with a tiny drawing that depicted an empty chamber and an arrow that pointed *in*, but this was truly beside the point. The point at the moment being that the chamber I had was full and the cartridge that fully filled it was refusing to snap *out.* Thus I became stranded on the desert isle of the Help Line (also known as the Hell Line) where 70 hours later (all right, but it was *two*) I was finally handed the secret: tilt the thing *up* before attempting to pull it *out.* And not only that, but the way to insert the new one was: tilt the thing *up* before attempting to push it *in.*

Three hours of sweating to the tune of Offensive Oldies when a short clear instruction could have shortened the time to zilch.

Or to put that another way, instructions are important. People consult instructions when they don't know diddly-squat and you must never assume they do. Instructions have to be clear. Just because *you* know the part about tilting up, you can't assume that your reader does. Spell it all out. Further, spell it out as you'd spell it out to your grandma—in plain, simple, clean, kind, non-technical English— meaning English that sounds human.

Here's another nasty example that arrived with my VCR—the putative instructions for How to Set the Clock:

1) Push Action to set clock. 2) Press ▲ or ▼ to select month. 3) Press ▶ to set your selection. 4) Repeat 2 and 3 to set date, year, time. 5) Press Action to start clock. 6) Press Action again to exit.

Clear, right? Nope, wrong. The only remote buttons that read ▲ and ▼ are for *Channel* up and down, and pushing them will get you a headache and little else. Further, while the symbol on the "Play" button is ▶, this too is misleading. The answer, thanks to 70 more hours of seeking Help is that "Play" (with the ▶ symbol) actually stands for ▲ (up), and "Stop" (with the ■ symbol) actually stands for ▼ (down), and finally, "Fast Forward" (whose symbol is ▶▶ double-barreled) is actually used for ▶ Set.

So, you may start to wonder, *why couldn't they say so?*

Well, in a way, they did. In exquisitely teensy type, in a place where you'd never look for it, they offered a little key. ("Play"= ▲.) But why did they need the key? Why couldn't they offer you— right within the instructions—

2) Select the month. (Press "Play" to move to an earlier month and "Stop" to move to a later one.)

Before you commit instructions, do [whatever it is] yourself. Note how you're doing it— a baby step at a time— and then offer the steps in order. As Thoreau would have summarized it:

SIMPLIFY, SIMPLIFY.

The absolute paradigm of fail-safe instruction, and the one I'd urge you to follow is (of all things)— a cookbook. Look:

Pumpkin Soup
(4 one-cup servings)

3 cups of milk	*1 Tbsp butter*
3 cups of canned pumpkin	*2 Tbsp brown sugar*
1 cup of minced ham	*salt, pepper, nutmeg, cinnamon*

1) Heat the milk in a saucepan. Just before it's boiling, turn off the flame.

2) Add the pumpkin and stir until smooth.

3) Add, in order, the butter, sugar, spices (to taste), and the ham, stirring till blended.

4) Heat slowly, but do not boil. When hot, serve at once

Here's an interesting exercise. Write the instructions for opening a can with an old-fashioned, hand-held turn-the-key opener. Take your instructions now and go open a can. Could you do it from your instructions and *only* from your instructions? What steps did you leave out? What portions were unclear? And now instruct your grandmother in how to change an ink cartridge, or how to send an email. (If your grandmother's a genius or an Intel executive, explain it to Spot, the dog.)

A FINAL NOTE ON INSTRUCTIONS: BEWARE AMBIGUITY.

A word has a meaning (a rose is a rose is a rose) but even "rose" has a couple of meanings. (The wind rose in the forest. The couch potatoes, the rabble, and the murder rate rose.) Even "is" can become confusing, as we're famously forced to know.[3] And if "is" can be indeterminate, then so can anything else. Ambiguity, as it happens, isn't always up to the writer since the reader is half the game. But the writer remains obliged to help the reader to unequivocally find the meaning the writer meant.

This occasionally calls for role play, where the writer is forced to ask himself, assuming the role of the reader: *Are there other ways to interpret this?* If so, and if your hypothetical reader isn't a dunce, then you're obligated to fix it.

Let's go for another example:

The company you're working for is planning a big event, one that's set for the following Thursday. A memo crosses your desk:

Please prepare a press release for the media on Thursday.

Without a decisive context, this could mean a couple of things.

On Thursday, please prepare a press release for the media.

Or: *Please prepare a release on [the subject of] Thursday's rally.*

Or: *Please prepare a release that we can hand out to the media at the site of Thursday's event.*

Any of these has logic: Please wait till Thursday when the details will be complete./ Please do it now so we can get the news to the press and hope they'll cover the big event./ Please prepare something we can hand to them if they come.

IT'S NOT UP TO YOUR READER TO INTUIT YOUR TRUE MEANING. YOUR WORDS HAVE TO SAY IT.

3 And for those too young to remember it, the grammar lesson in question came from President Bill Clinton, throwing curves at a grand jury. Asked about the statement of his putative past mistress that there "absolutely *is* no sex of any kind," he resourcefully responded that its verity lay entirely in the problematical fog of "what the meaning of *is* is." "If *is*," he instructed, "means is and never was, well, that would be one thing. On the other hand, if *is* means there isn't any now, then the statement would be correct." Of course, this example goes to purposeful ambiguity; our subject is inadvertence.

14.
WRITER'S BLOCK
(JUST TOO HORRIBLE FOR WORDS)

Ummmm..........................

Err...

..........To every good pilgrim on the tortuous road to progress, there eventually befalls the forced stop at the stone wall. What's worst about the wall is, there's no way around it. Cliff on the one side, swamp on the other. The wall, like a mismated love affair or the measles, simply has to be gotten *over.*

How to get over it relates to how it began or, more precisely, *when* it began, because the *when* prefigures the *why*. In general, though, the three most popular kinds of structures are, 1) I can't get started, 2) I can't go on, and 3) I haven't the foggiest idea what I'm doing.

Let's approach them one at a time.

I Can't Get Started

This is known as procrastination, of which there are two kinds: normal procrastination and mortal procrastination. Each has a different cause. Normal procrastination is the normal human reaction to the threat of a blank page. Its origins, so they tell me, can be traced to the first hominid who stared at a cave wall and, uncertain of what to do about it, brutally banged his head until a thousand millennia later when he finally sketched a bear. The moral, it soon occurred to him, was Wait till the last minute. This lesson was learned well, passing down through the generations like the secrets of wheels and fire. Its corollary, however, which was Wait till you know what you're doing, isn't really a bad idea.

Which gets us back to The Process. What you hope to do in The Process is to learn what you hope to do, and get some markers on how to do it. Then too, if you're very lucky, you'll have doodled how to begin.

How to begin is the first hurdle. For most writers, the magic breakthrough is the moment they've got the lead, which can either be the attack point (the thrust of the opening gambit) or the actual opening line. Just a single passable sentence, a mere fragment that's just-so, can be the rocket that leaps the wall. Ernest Hemingway, so it's said, wrote atrociously, though doggedly, every morning for days on end before he finally got the "one true sentence" that calmed the Muses and allowed him to start the book. Article-writers, too, say the lead is the work's foundation, that without it there's nothing else, though it's certainly true that the lead provides the writer with hope and cheer. "Oh, look!" he says of his sentence. "There's a chance I can really write!"

The right beginning, to put it gently, rarely ever comes at the start. You have to sidle your way into it. Make the sidling part of The Process.

Here's another couple of tricks:

Set yourself a start date—a generous number of days before the fateful day of your deadline. Cancel any appointments. Pencil X's across your calendar from starting day to the end.

Allow yourself vices. This is certainly not the time to quit smoking or start a diet.

Eliminate distractions. If you need to get out of your garret, you may leave it to go for a walk or a lonely lunch at the local diner just as long as you carry with you an empty surface on which to write. Think idly about your work or think profoundly about nothing. This is done in the wistful hope that your subconscious will do the job.

Write something (anything) Else. If you can't start your thesis, write a birthday poem to your cat. Write a letter to Aunt Matilda. In other words, write. Writing can breed writing.

Finally, if you're desperate, read an article, book or poem by any writer who knocks you out. Good writing can be contagious.

Mortal procrastination is, however, a different game— one that plays to your darkest fancies. (I'm not up to the job. If I do it, I'll only fail. If I fail, I'm disgraced forever.) All of which is a totally perfect setup to never try. (You don't try it, you can't fail.) Though, of course, if you never try it, then your failure is guaranteed and, even worse, your failure to try it is the fatal mark of the wimp. Remind yourself that failure to even try is a failure too— just a more cowardly version. Remind yourself also that your consummate fear of failure is the reason why you'll succeed.

There are, however, two other reasons you can't start that may, in fact, have a leg to stand on: Try, as you really have, you simply don't believe in the job. You don't believe that it's worth doing. You don't believe in the thing at all. You are intellectually balking. The question to then ask yourself is, Is there a way out? Can you still refuse the assignment? If there isn't and if you can't, there's nothing left but Return to Go: The Process, the Start Date, and all of the other hints.

Finally, of course, there's the plain You don't *want* to. You know, of course, that you should— you may even know that you must— but your inclinations are purely other. (You can lead your horse to Oughta, but you can't make it think.) Again, if you truly can't free yourself of the burden, then attempt to sweeten the pot. Bribe yourself. Assure yourself you'll like it once you've begun. Or even better, change the assignment into something you want to do.

I Can't Go On

So there you are, 150 pages into your thesis, 2 pages into your article, 5 pages into your pitch, or nearly finished with your report and then alarmingly, *Screech-thud.* You are staring straight at The Wall. Suddenly, inexplicably, you can't see where you're going. Or perhaps, looking behind you, you hate wherever you've been. This, too, is, alas, normal and may succumb to a cogent plan. The first step of the plan is:

Identify Your Impasse.

Your impasse will usually come in one of the following forms (or, God help you, in all four).

You hate whatever you've written. You detest your actual words which are unconvincing and uninspired and you can't advance till you've doubled back. If that's the problem, then double back. Paragraph by paragraph, rewrite what you've come to hate until you suddenly come to love it. Love— even love of your own sentences— conquers all. (Could you actually scrap the project now and silence your lovely words?) And besides, they've now provided a firm foundation on which to build.

But this is truly a matter of temperament. A ream full of rotten writing doesn't ruin the path for some, and many others, spurning temptation, take their lesson from Lot's Wife— looking backward can freeze you solid. Don't reread it. Stay on the run.

On the turf of The Happy Middle, you can work it in two directions. At the end of a day's adventures, when you feel that you're written out, take a coffee break or a shower and, reinforcing yourself, reluctantly read it over and gently polish. You can give it a second polish at the start of the second day, when the polishing keeps you limber. You can think of the second polish as the warm-up before the race, or as the gardener of firm ground.

You can't—you can absolutely *not*—write at all. Decent writing is often hard, but there are times when it's harder than others— when the words refuse to be written because the words refuse to occur— but at least you're in good company. There isn't a writer born who hasn't suffered the Dreadful Week when nothing happens that isn't drivel, and the choices are down to two. You can manufacture your drivel in the hopes that you'll fix it later while at least you're covering ground, or you can madly embrace your demons.

If your deadline allows for madness, walk your monster around the block, but do it firmly and have a plan. A monster without a master is like a river without a dam. Take control of it; rein it in. Demand of yourself a small daily doable set of goals. ("Tomorrow I'll tough it out and write one passable passage"/ "one passable paragraph"/ "one passable line"/ "find one appropriate adjective.") Do whatever you've said. Remain, chained to the spot, till you've delivered on what you've promised, or till a vein explodes in your neck.

If a vein explodes in your neck, propose a tinier goal for the morrow— could you write an *eighth* of a sentence; could you manage the word "the"?

Painful writing, sad as it is, isn't even the direst fate that can ever befall a writer; there's the curse of the *je ne sais quoi*, which is French for the Hideous Whaddayacallit that doesn't admit to a name. This perhaps is the commonest Block.

Something's wrong, but you don't know what. Or something's wrong and you do know what, except you haven't the wit to cure it. Either way, it's back to The Process. Specifically, Step One, in which the point of your random jottings is to name your elusive glitch. Something, you feel, is wrong. So what do you feel it is? Where (at what point) do you feel that you went astray? Read it over. Look for the spot. Peel it back to the point of trouble. What was wrong with it after that? What on earth could you do instead? If the problem's the organization, then consider another path. Consider another outline. Or several other outlines. Follow them where they lead. *Diagram* where they lead. Remember, you're not writing now; you're analyzing your work.

Is the problem a lack of clarity? Is it structurally too diffuse? Once again, try another outline. Make a list of your salient points. Cut the clutter you've stuck between them. Plot a sensible road ahead.

So, too, if you know the problem. Make an idle list of solutions. Then consider their ramifications. Where would each of your answers lead? Still unhappy? Quit for the day.

A good pause is another weapon. You can think of your stalled project as you'd think of a stalled car. By repeatedly pumping the pedal, all you're doing is flooding the engine (with the engine being your head). Something mindless can be the cure. Something mindless but not distracting. Physical labor can rest the mind. Plant your garden. Clean your garage. Paper your kitchen. Or all three. Your epiphany, like the thunderbolt of unexpected romance, may emerge from your lack of thinking. I'm suggesting this from experience. Once, when stuck on a project, I replaced the floor in the kitchen, then replaced the floor in the bathroom, and was deeply and rather desperately into papering all the closets when I suddenly knew the problem so I suddenly knew the cure.

If nothing above helps, SOS to a smart friend. And preferably to a friend who understands what you're trying to do and who perhaps has done it himself. Refrain from asking your mother, lover, roommate, sibling or spouse.

Be Ready To Be Ruthless.

If you pinpoint your error and decide (to your terror) that it's 70 pages back, peel back to the point of error, discard the 70 pages (doesn't matter how much you love them) and resume on the right track.

If the problematic passage is your seven favorite lines or your exquisitely sharp analogy or the joke that you couldn't resist, or even the point that you couldn't elaborate on as skillfully as you'd wished, say goodbye to it, nonetheless. Life is choices, and some are hard. The screenwriter, novelist and essayist William Goldman summed it up with his harsh but unarguable advice: "You have to be willing to kill your darlings."

I Haven't The Foggiest Idea What I'm Doing.

You've been sailing along breezily and, wham! you're at sea. Suddenly, unexpectedly, you seem to have lost your polestar. It's not that you decidedly dislike whatever you're doing, it's just that you're considerably confused about what it *is*. Or if it *is*, in fact, anything. Certainly, it's pages and pages of lovely words but they haven't begun to accumulate; the pitch/article/essay doesn't seem to have taken shape.

This, too, is a common feeling. Many writers, famous and classic, have reported the same fog. "I'm in the midst of a novel which I simply have never grasped," D.H. Lawrence wrote to a friend. "There I am at page 145 and I've no notion what it's about."

What Lawrence actually meant was, the thing hadn't cohered— the parts hadn't come together. The chapters were only chapters, but they hadn't become a book.

Once again, this is fairly common. Writing— at least writing something even vaguely ambitious, whether fiction or nonfiction— is like making a mayonnaise.

Have you ever made mayonnaise?

First you break a couple of raw egg yolks into a bowl. Then slo-o-o-o-wly, pouring straight from the bottle, you add oil while simultaneously stirring madly. That's it. You keep doing it, and doing it, and doing it and...all you seem to have fashioned is a bowlful of oily eggs. This is totally gross and disgusting. Still, undaunted, you carry on. Adding oil, stirring with fury, finding all that you've got in front of you now is... *more* oily eggs. You think, "I'm doing this wrong." You think, wondering vaguely about the state of your carpal tunnel, that you might as well throw it out. And then, wham! all of a sudden, just bam!, in the blink of an eye, your messy liquid becomes a solid, or, more commonly put, it gels. This gel is your mayonnaise. And from that moment forward, as you're pouring, stirring, and pouring, you're miraculously creating ever *more* mayonnaise.

Lawrence's oily eggs became the novel *Women In Love.*

You can take that as inspiration— or at least up to a point. Raw persistence can be the answer.

Another cause of confusion, quite aside from a crisis of faith, is a simple crisis of thought. You haven't, perhaps, defined what it is you're trying to say, so no wonder you can't say it. Or perhaps, even worse, what you thought you wanted to say doesn't seem to be holding true. Again, you're in good company. A world-famous economist told an interviewer from C-SPAN that he reached a similar point as he was writing his recent book. "By the time I got to Chapter Five," he said mordantly, "I discovered that many views I'd held in Chapter Three were false."

Through the process of writing—and writing and writing—he'd knocked down his own thesis and discovered a finer thought. Or, to put that another way: he wrote his way into the problem and then wrote his way out of it. Or *thought* his way out of the problem through the physical task of writing.

This will often be your solution. Or not, as the case may be. Which gets us to the final, most disheartening part of The Block:

KNOWING WHEN TO QUIT.

Sometimes it is, as you've deeply suspected, hopeless. You and your material simply aren't a match. Your writing is really lousy. Your inspiration is really dead. The idea, which in its bright shiny beginnings had seemed terrific, falls apart when it hits the page. (The devil was in the details and the details refused to play.)

It also might be the case that the material itself just resists organization and requires complete rethinking which you're too exhausted to do. At least at the moment. Perhaps at another time...

Yes, you have come a cropper. The project, indeed, failed. Not you, just the project. It failed from its own glitches— from the problems you couldn't foresee. You have probably learned a lesson, but the lesson isn't defeat, it's a lesson about writing, about projects with fatal flaws, about the limits of wit to save them, and the human limits of will.

The author Joyce Carol Oates had this to say on the subject and I'll leave you with her words.

"I would suggest that if a writer truly experiences a block, he should totally abandon the work and write something else. When a writer deals with his true subject, when he allows himself to give verbal expression to something truly important to him, there's no question of not writing, only a question of there being too few hours in the day."

Or, to put that another way:

**When You've Tried At Least Half-a-dozen Ways
To Skin A Cat And It's Still Got It's Fur On,
Try Another Cat.**

LaVergne, TN USA
27 December 2009
168124LV00006B/182/P